Asking for Wisdom

Maximizing Your Time with Mentors

by
Craig Thompson

Published by Thompson Publishers

The Mentoring Revolution Series: Book Two

Thompson Publishers
thompsonpublishers.com

Asking for Wisdom: Maximizing Your Time with Mentors
The Mentoring Revolution Series: Book Two
Copyright © 2019 by Craig Thompson

Requests for information should be address to:
Thompson Publishers, PO Box 2605, Cleveland TN 37320-2605

ISBN: 978-1-64407-004-8 [softcover]
ISBN: 978-1-64407-005-5 [ebook]

All rights reserved. No part of this book may be reproduced, stored in a retrieval system, or transmitted in any form or by any means -- electronic, mechanical, photocopy, recording, or any other -- except for brief quotations printed in reviews, without the permission of the publisher.

Scripture taken from the New King James Version®. Copyright © 1982 by Thomas Nelson. Used by permission. All rights reserved.

Cover design Craig Thompson © 2019.

Printed in the USA.
First printing.

"Getting good advice from some people
is like drawing water from a deep well,
but a man of understanding
knows how to draw it out."
Proverbs 20:5

Other Books by the Same Author

The Mentoring Revolution Series
52 Godly Mentors Parent's Planning Guide
How To Be a Mentor for a Day
Nurturing Your Children Through Mentors
The Mentoring Revolution Small Group Curriculum

Other Works
Preaching Through Proverbs: A Collection of Sermons by the Pastors of Central Africa

To my parents, who never berated me for asking so many questions, and to my children who have continued the tradition of asking many questions of their parents.

Contents

Preface
Making Proper Introductions 1
The Value of Heeding Advice 4
Active Listening 8
The Importance of Asking Questions 10
Preparing for Your Meeting 13
The Five W's 16
What? 20
When? 24
Where? 28
Why? 32
The Big H 37
Setup and Follow-Up Questions 42
The Protocol of Questioning 48
Questioning Authority 51
Mining for Gold 56
Drilling for Oil 61
Digging a Well 66
Putting It All Together 70
Acknowledgments 73
Comments 74
Errata 75
Bonus Content 79

Preface

I wrote this book for one purpose: to help young men and women learn the lessons which I have taught my own children about how to maximize their time with mentors. My children begin a journey when they are 13 years old. They meet with one mentor each week for a full year. As they travel through that journey, I coach them on how to find the nuggets of truth that can help to change their own lives. The core of what I teach my own children during this year is how to ask really good questions. I do that because I understand that one of the best ways we can acquire wisdom is by tapping into the storehouse of knowledge of other people. Good questions are the key to getting into that storehouse.

Whether you are a youth seeking instruction or a parent/teacher who wants to instruct others on how to maximize their time with a mentor, this book is for you. It doesn't matter if you have a series of meetings with a mentor, a full day, one hour or even just a few minutes, what you learn in this book will help you to get more out of that time if you are willing to put it into practice. Each chapter builds upon the content learned in the previous chapters. Therefore, you should read this book from start to finish.

If you are using this book in conjunction with one of our mentoring programs such as "52 Godly Men/Women" or our curriculum for churches and groups, I recommend that you focus on reading and practicing what you learn in one chapter per week. Those programs are intentionally spread out over 26, 39 or 52 weeks, and the habit of practicing the information will help you to grow in the skills we look at in each chapter.

There are numerous examples given throughout the book. Use them! Each of the main chapters has ten sample questions.

You may use those verbatim in your own meetings with mentors, or you can alter them to meet your needs. As you practice, you will add to your own personal repertoire until you have a good feel for using your questions as a tool.

Let me encourage you to remember two things in your meetings with every mentor. You should set obtainable goals and seek to define measurable steps. If you want to become a licensed plumber, a heavy equipment operator, a neurosurgeon or anything else, you need to assess whether this is truly obtainable for you and, if so, determine what steps will move you closer to your goal. The same holds true of all the other aspects of our lives. You may want to be a successful parent, a world traveler, an author of books or a person of integrity. Each of these is a real goal which requires its own individual actions and steps in order to be realized. When you meet with mentors, the questions you ask should relate to your life goals. While it is enjoyable and worthwhile just to get to know people, at the end of the day you must ask yourself if you made progress or lost ground on your goals in your personal interactions with others.

The effectiveness of what you learn here will only be as potent as your willingness to actually use it. In the lives of my own children, I have watched them grow and become transformed by their time spent with mentors as they journeyed through the 52 Godly Men and 52 Godly Women programs. What you are reading here definitely works. My oldest children have had a chance to write and speak about their experiences, and years after working through the mentoring program, they still recognize the impact it had on their lives.

A note on faith. In this book, I make occasional references to my faith in Jesus Christ. While I realize that not everyone shares that faith, I am confident that the principles outlined in this book are still useful to whomever reads this book.

Neither am I apologetic for the references; they're not going to bite you if you don't agree with them. As a father looking for good mentors to meet with my children, I have found some of the best men and women of character to be those who are doing their best to follow the biblical example set by Jesus. Hypocrites aside—and they do exist—there are plenty of men and women living out their daily lives without pretense, with wisdom and with a genuine love for others. These are the people I encourage you to try to find as mentors in your own life.

As with all of my books, I welcome your feedback. It allows me to add material or clarify sections. Comments on this book can be sent to askingforwisdom@walkwithgod.com.

Chapter One
Making Proper Introductions

"Hello!" Proper greetings are the foundation upon which relationships can be built in informal or business settings. If you are going to meet with mentors, some of them may be people you do not know personally. Did you know that how you introduce yourself the first time to new acquaintances will help to form an opinion of you which may last for years? Right or wrong, their view of you will be impacted largely by their first impressions of you.

This is why it is so important to learn how to simply say, "hello" the best way possible. In this chapter, we're going to talk about how to do that the right way. We will also talk about some bad habits which you can learn to avoid.

First, let's talk about your face. Your face should have a smile on it. That's one of the things people will remember about you long after you part ways. "He smiled when he met me." So, make a conscious effort and begin to develop the habit of smiling when you are introduced to someone new. While it may seem funny to think about, you should not break into a silly grin (and that goes especially for boys meeting girls they want to know better). Don't force a large, fake smile. People can spot a phony.

The easiest thing to do is to force the corners of your mouth upward into a smile. When you do that, your brain releases chemicals which can relax your body and lower your heart rate and blood pressure. The simple act of smiling helps you to actually feel happier. Try it.

After you smile, make eye contact with the person. This is easier for some people than others. Some cultures actually teach their people that looking into the eyes of someone in authority is disrespectful. In our culture, we show respect by looking into the eyes of the other person. The easiest way to do this is to smile, make eye contact and hold eye contact briefly while you begin the process of shaking hands.

Do not bulge your eyes out or stare at the person as if he is a new toy. If the person dresses completely different from you, don't be distracted by the clothing. If he is richer, poorer, physically deformed, has a large nose or missing teeth, don't focus on any of these. Eye contact lets you focus on the windows of his soul.

The third step is to speak your own name by way of greeting. This is as simple as saying, "John Smith" or "I'm John Smith" or "My name is John Smith." Depending upon who speaks first, the other person will typically reciprocate this by offering his name.

The fourth step is to extend your right hand for a handshake. You can start this while you are still speaking. You may be left-handed, but in our culture, handshakes are done with the right hand. The handshake should be a brief, but firm grip. You learn by practice what is a common way of shaking hands.

Do not offer a limp fish handshake. Do not squeeze the other person's hand in a death grip. Do not slide a stiff hand in like a piece of wood. If your hands are sticky, filthy or generally dirty, it is acceptable to say, "Please excuse me a moment" while you use a rag, cloth or your clothes to wipe or dust off your hands. This says to the other person that you are regarding him with respect and that this meeting is more than a formality. It says that you value him.

After you shake hands, close out your introduction by stating something like the following, "Bob, it's a pleasure to meet you." You can repeat the person's name once or twice aloud to help to remember it like this, "Bob Allen … Bob Allen. Bob, I'm glad to meet you." There are entire books and courses which can teach you how to remember a person's name. But make it a point to repeat the person's name out loud and then internally in order to help to remember it as you make conversation.

You should practice what we've learned. You can try this with a family member or friend. First, stand up and turn to your friend. Smile. Then make eye contact. Take turns stating your names as you begin to extend your hand for a handshake. Keep smiling. After names have been exchanged, let the person know that you are glad to get to know him. Now find someone else to practice on. Keep practicing until the actions become a habit.

Practicing this may seem awkward at first. Push through anyway. It will pay off in your relationships. Just this past week, I had an opportunity to visit a relative I had not seen in a long time. I had with me my son who had been through this training almost a year earlier. During our visit, my cousin's wife remarked that my twelve-year-old son had greeted her like an adult. She was very impressed with how he presented himself. As you work on this skill, keep in mind that you never get a second chance to make a good first impression.

Application

Make it a point to practice this daily, several times a day over the next week. Use your family and close friends to help you with this. If you meet someone new this week, be sure to implement what you have learned in this lesson.

Chapter Two
The Value of Heeding Advice

Long ago, there were three friend who were traveling in a distant country. As nightfall approached, they began to set up camp for the night. As they were cooking their supper of limited rations, an old man slowly came out of the darkness. He was bent over from age.

He looked at the travelers and asked if they had any food which they could spare for him. The friends were not stingy, and they each quickly took some food from their own portions in order to offer their guest a generous portion.

After they all had eaten and were getting ready to retire for the night, the old man asked their destination. When they told him, he replied that he was very familiar with their route. He said, "Because you have been kind to me, I would like to show kindness to you." The friends said that he didn't owe them anything, but the man replied, "No. You have shown me hospitality, an old man and a stranger. So I will tell you a secret that few know. In two days journey, you will arrive at a river. It is important that you not cross the river by day. Instead, wait until night time. At night, once every 99 years, the water recedes, and you will be able to cross it easily. That night is just two nights away."

The friends had never heard of a river like this, but they listened politely. What the man said next was very strange. "When you cross the river, you will feel yourself going down, and then you will reach the flat bottom of the riverbed. Once you reach the bottom of the river, kneel down and begin picking up the rocks around you. Fill your pockets and bags with as many rocks as you can. As you travel onward, once the morning light comes, open your bags and pockets and look. You will be very happy, and you will also be very sad."

At this, the friends had to work hard to not smile and show their amusement at what the old man had said. They turned in for the night. When they awoke the next morning, the old man had already departed. They talked about his riddle and had a few good laughs at what he had said. However, in two days, at evening time, they heard the sound of rushing water not too far ahead of them. They pushed on and came to the edge of a river just as the sun was beginning to set.

Could it be true? They wondered if what the old man had told them was accurate. Would the river dry up at night, allowing them to cross over without having to fight the strong current?

They decided to keep watch. During the first watch, the friend who was on duty heard the roar of the water begin to diminish. He told the second friend when he took over. During his watch, the river grew completely quiet. He ventured to the edge and listened. He took stones and threw them out as far as he could. But the stones only clattered when they hit. The river was dry.

Quickly, he awoke his companions. They broke camp, packed and made their way to the riverbank. Excitedly, they began walking down the slope. The old man was right after all! They were able to cross a big obstacle with no trouble at all.

When they reached the bottom, they were about to begin their climb up the other side when one friend remembered what else the old man had said. "Do you think we should really pick up some of the rocks and put them in our bags and pockets?" It sounded crazy even as he said it. But one of the friends said, "Even if we only do it to honor him for making our journey easier, I think we should."

So, they each knelt down and felt around them. There were numerous rocks of different sizes and weights. Two of the friends put a few rocks in their pockets and a few in their packs just to honor the old man's good advice he had given them. One friend, however, decided to do exactly as the old man had said. After all, he had been right about the river. In spite of how crazy it sounded, he stuffed his pockets full of rocks and filled his pack until it was bulging with rocks. It was difficult carrying the loaded pack up the steep riverbank; in fact, the other two friends threw many of the heavier rocks out of their packs. Once they made it to the other side, they set up camp and rested soundly.

The next morning, the sun awoke them to a new day. The friends began to make preparations for breakfast. One of them reached into his bag to get his salt. Suddenly he shouted, "Look! See what I have in my pack!" The other two friends ran over and looked. There, sitting at the top of his bag were the largest diamonds, rubies and emeralds they had even seen in their lives.

Quickly, the other two friends ran to their packs. When they opened them, they discovered that they, too, had picked up treasure. When they reached into the pockets of their clothes, they found the same and other kinds of precious stones. They were overjoyed! They had instant wealth in their hands, and it had been free!

And then it hit them. Why had they taken the largest stones out of their packs and thrown them away? What kind of stones had they been: a two-pound diamond, a four-pound ruby, a five-pound emerald? Their packs and their pockets were nowhere near full. The old man had told them to pick up as many rocks as they could, but they had not really believed him. Yes, they were very happy. But they were also very sad. They wished they could do it over. Only one of the friends had listened and obeyed the old man, and his pack and pockets were filled to overflowing with glittering riches.

The friends stayed by the river for three weeks and listened every night to see if the river would stop flowing again, but it never did. The old man said that this was a once in a lifetime happening. He was right. With a mixture of happiness and sadness, they finally broke camp and continued on their journey to their destination.

This story is a parable for you. You are the travelers, the friends on a journey. Each of the mentors you have the opportunity to meet with are like the old man. They have wisdom and knowledge about the path you are on. They want to help you cross obstacles as easily as possible. They also want to tell you things which will make your life richer and fuller. Sometimes, what you hear spoken is a once in a lifetime nugget of wisdom which can change your life forever. Whether or not you listen and act on their advice is up to you. If you listen and act on their godly counsel, you will be happy as you continue on your journey. And, if you don't listen at all or only listen half-heartedly, you will be very sad.

Application

Over the next few days, make it a point to focus your attention when people are speaking to you. Find one particular idea or truth which you can act on that day or in the next few days and try it. Truth which isn't applied to your life is useless to you.

Chapter Three
Active Listening

In the last chapter, we talked about the travelers who picked up the stones in the riverbed. In that story, the friends had to take an action by reaching out and gathering the stones in the darkness, an action which required a little effort on their part. But the truth is, sometimes there are precious stones which lie on the surface ready for the taking, if we are willing to simply reach out and grab them.

This is similar to active listening. Active listening is different from just sitting there with a blank look on your face or staring off into space while you allow your mind to wander. Active listening means that you have focused your attention on the speaker in order to glean the most information possible from him.

If you have not worked to develop this skill, there are several actions you can take to begin the process of disciplining your mind to be able to listen actively. The first step is to silence the electronic devices around you. This could be a cell phone, a TV, a gaming console, an audio player or a computer. Turn it down or just turn it off. People flatter themselves by telling others that they can multitask, but at the base level, if you are paying attention to a screen, you are not listening with your full attention. Call it foolish, call it a waste of time or call it just plain rude, but don't call it multitasking.

The second action you can take to begin listening actively is to keep a paper and pen handy. This is useful for dealing with distractions. Often, while you are learning to train your mind to listen, you will be distracted by a thought of a job you need to do, a task which was forgotten or something similar. What do you do? Dwell on it and let it distract you for 1-2 minutes?

No. Write it down briefly on the paper and then forget about it. Go back to listening. Some people are distracted by visual movements around them. If that is you, try closing your eyes as you listen. It may help you block out the distractions around you.

Another tool to aid you in the habit of active listening is taking notes. The act of writing down the lessons you are hearing can help you absorb them more fully. Note taking is itself a discipline, but you can get started by simply writing down key quotes, parts of phrases, references to books, scripture verses, events or key people. This is also a good time to write down questions which are spurred in your mind by what you are hearing. Even if you cannot ask the speaker your question, you can research the answer later on your own.

Finally, remember to pray and ask God to help you to learn to listen better. His Word instructs us to be swift to hear, so that is a prayer you know He will answer.

In closing, listening, really listening, is a skill which will serve you well the rest of your life. It will be the foundation of your deepest relationships. It not only can add wealth and benefits to you, but it may also one day save your life or the lives of those you love.

Application

Begin the habit of keeping a pen and paper with you or nearby so that you can take notes. If your parents or employer give you a task, write down the steps which you need to complete the task. If you have an opportunity, read back your list and ask if you heard correctly what you are supposed to do.

Chapter Four
The Importance of Asking Questions

How many of you have heard the old saying, "You never learn anything by talking, only by listening"? Well, that's only partly true. You can learn something by talking — if you know how to ask questions.

Asking questions is a vital tool to make the most of any mentoring opportunity. Whether you are spending time weekly with a mentor or whether you happen to see one of your heroes at a conference or banquet, the ability to ask a good, solid question can open up a world of truth to you in the answers you receive from the wise.

Over the next few chapters, we are going to learn how to ask questions. By the end of these lessons, you will have the tools to enable you to interview anyone, anywhere, at any time. But, another old saying states, "You have to learn to walk before you can run." So there are some basic principles about asking questions which you need to initially learn.

First, when you begin to ask questions of your mentors, start with your interests. If you love sports, there is nothing wrong with asking your mentor if he likes sports, too, or which sports he prefers to play. If you like music, ask which type of composer or singer or band he likes the most. Asking questions based on your interest allows you to participate in the response you receive. You have something invested in the person's answer because you are talking about something which matters to you. Sometimes in life, such as in a job interview, the ability to be personal is the key to having a door open. Rather than always feeling like you have to don a reporter's hat and pull out a notepad, having the ability to just talk about common interests is very important.

Second, ask questions about the person's family. If the person has a family, this is usually a topic of dear importance to him. Ask to see photos of the mentor's spouse or children if they mention them. Ask their names and ages. Parents love to talk about their children. Plus, they will be glad you asked.

Third, don't be afraid to ask what you might think are obvious questions. If you want to know how someone became a professional athlete, ask "How did you get from being someone like me to being someone like you?" Then listen and takes notes.

Finally, let me mention another old saying: "There's no such thing as a dumb question." This is only partially true. We've all heard some pretty dumb questions in our time. Having someone stand in front of a huge clock and ask, "What time is it?" simply shows that the person isn't paying attention (or doesn't know the basics of how to tell time). If your mentor has explained to you how to tie a knot ten different ways, don't ask, "How do you tie a knot?" Dumb questions arise from not listening, not paying attention and generally not being engaged in the world around you.

Where I agree with this old saying is when someone feels intimidated to ask a question because he doesn't really understand a word, a phrase or an idea. This is when you need to realize that asking a question in order to learn something is never dumb. Do not be put off by your peers or enemies who might laugh at you for asking a question. If you do not understand something, ask and ask again until you do understand it. Remember, you are the one you are gaining knowledge for, not for your enemies. If they never understand what is being taught or discussed, that is their problem. The simplest way to handle this in a mentoring relationship or in school or with your family is to look at the person doing the talking and state, "I am having trouble understanding this. I want to learn. Will you explain it again?"

Your ability to grow and learn the secrets of the world around you begin with curiosity and wonder in your own heart and mind. As soon as you begin to let your curiosity wonder, you will begin to ask questions. And once you start down the path of asking questions, a world of knowledge awaits you.

Application

Take a few moments to think of an answer to this question: "What is something I have always wanted to know about or understand?" Once you have picked a subject, topic or idea, then ask this follow up question: "What person do I know who would be able to help me learn more about this?" Then go to that person and tell him that you would like to know more about that topic. Ask the question, "Would you be willing to share some of what you know about this topic with me?" It could be something as simple as how to tie a particular type of knot. It could be how to prepare a certain type of meal or dish. It could be the particle theory in chemistry. What matters is that you act on this lesson by beginning to ask a question in order to actually learn something new. Start today.

Chapter Five
Preparing for Your Meeting

My children generally begin meeting with mentors when they are thirteen. Because they are thirteen and not thirty or forty or sixty, I realize that they do not have the life experience necessary to even begin to understand what all the questions are which they should ask of a mentor. In your own life, it can take some pressure off of you if you realize that where you are now in life is not the version of you twenty years in the future. You simply cannot ask questions which you do not know to ask. This chapter is designed to help you begin thinking about what you know about your mentor.

One question to ask yourself is if there are any character traits you admire about this person. Sometimes I pick mentors for my children based on dominant positive character traits. I would like my children to be exposed to men and women who are overflowing with love, joy, peace, patience or other personality features which are desirable. (For a good list of traits to look for in mentors, see Galatians 5:22-23 in the Bible.) Although some people naturally seem to excel in certain traits, to have them be such a strong part of a person's character usually means that they have spent time learning and developing those traits. I want my children to be able to ask, "How did you get such a strong, abiding peace in your life?" or "You are known as a very patient person. How did you get to be so patient?"

Take time to examine the mentor's family. Does the mentor have an especially strong marriage? Does the mentor have a strong relationship with his children? Are the children respectful, intelligent and emotionally healthy? You would then form questions around these types of topics.

Look at the mentor's involvement in the surrounding community. Does the mentor coach, volunteer in relief work or provide help to people on an individual basis? Ask him what drove him to become involved, why he chose his particular field of service and how he integrates volunteer service with who he is as a person.

Is there anything related to business or financial management that you want to ask this mentor? Is he particularly good with investments? Does he own rental property? A young teenager may be focused on asking questions like, "How can I make money?" but as you learn more about life, your questions should become something like, "How do you take a company from $100,000 a year in sales to $1,000,000 or $10,000,000 in sales?"

A person's spirituality should also be a subject of your focus. Ask yourself the question, "What do I admire about this mentor's walk with God?" More than one of the women I asked to meet with my daughters were known as women of prayer. One of the men who met with my son has smuggled Bibles into Communist countries at great risk to himself. Other mentors have experienced great opposition without becoming bitter. Asking about a mentor's journey of faith can help answer questions which may arise in your own life, whether now or much later in life.

Application

When I meet with my children prior to taking them to a mentoring appointment as part of 52 Godly Men or 52 Godly Women, one of the main things we do is to prepare a working list of questions for them to ask. They have a pen and paper (or their notebook) ready. I usually begin by giving them some background information on the person just to set the context for their meeting and questions. Before you meet with your mentor, it would be helpful to ask your parents to help you with the same type of information. Ask them the above questions about the mentor. What they know about the mentor's business acumen, character traits or spirituality will likely be more detailed than what you know. Use that knowledge to add to your questions.

Chapter Six
The Five W's

For centuries, news reporters, lawyers and other learned men have valued five questions. Those questions are, "Who? What? When? Where? and Why?" In order for you to begin to learn more from your mentors, you need to learn the value of these questions and how to use them to your advantage. In these next five chapters, we will look at each one in detail.

Who? This question can be asked a variety of ways in order to learn from a mentor. Usually, the "who" question is used to learn about important relationships in a mentor's life. By learning about a mentor's key relationships, you can start to learn from their own mentors.

While that statement may not be clear at first glance, here is one example. If you ask your mentor the question, "Who are the two or three most influential people in your life?" then they will respond with two or three names. As you write down those names, you may find out that one or more of these people have written a book (or books). Or they may have videos or recordings of their teaching or interviews. This gives you the opportunity to read or listen to and then learn from the people who influenced your mentor.

So, when you ask the "who" question, focus on asking it in such a way that it actually leads you to information which will benefit you. Let's look at practical examples.

1. "Who was the greatest positive influence in your life?" Whether we ask for one or two or three, we are trying to

find out potential sources of wisdom. If you really respect someone's character, wisdom or knowledge, chances are that they were themselves impacted by other people who may still be alive or may have written books which can benefit you.

2. "Who gave you your first big opportunity in your career?" A question like this is designed to get a person to talk about not just a person but also a series of events which led to a breakthrough. It can unleash a good story.

3. "Who from history would you choose to talk to for one hour if you could meet anyone?" This is a tried and true question used by many interviewers. The point of this question is to learn more about who your mentor views as one of the most important, wisest or most influential person throughout history.

4. "Who are the people you read, study or learn from today?" As noted earlier, by asking this question, you can gather names which can lead you to books, interviews, videos or other resources which can help you to grow. Why not try to find the same sources of wisdom and knowledge as your mentor?

5. "Who was with you when you rescued the hostages?" This is an example of a specific question for a particular interview situation. The purpose is to allow the mentor to talk about an interaction of teamwork and how key relationships brought about a successful action. The same type of question could be asked for a scientific discovery or an invention or even a religious experience.

6. "Whom or what do you fear the most?" This question probably won't be answered truthfully by many people or won't be answered at all. But if you can get a frank answer, it can help you to understand motivations and the inner workings of a mentor's mind. (It also works well with the

follow-up question "why" or "why did you pick that" to dig deeper.)

7. "Whom do you love the most?" When asking this question to a godly mentor, much of the time the response may be "God." You may need to couch the question as: "Other than God, whom do you love the most?" As with the previous question, if answered frankly, this question can help you to understand more about the core motivations and decisions of a mentor.

8. "If you could pick anyone alive to be your mentor, whom would you pick?" This gives you a glimpse into areas of needed growth that your mentor sees in his own life. It also gives you a "best pick" of someone to follow up on for your own growth.

9. "Who has been your worst enemy?" or "Who has been one of your worst enemies?" This can be a dangerous question. It can cause a person to close up for a bit as they think about bad memories. They could even end the interview. However, if you can find a place to fit a question like this into a conversation, it can lead you into follow-up questions on how to handle conflict, how to deal with anger or bitterness and how to overcome adversity. Another way of asking a question like this is, "Who has caused some of your greatest conflict which you believe ultimately led to some of your greatest growth?"

10. "Who would you point out currently as someone who is living foolishly in our society or the world at large?" For mentors with a global or national grasp of issues, this can be an incredibly informative topic. Answers could range from movie stars to ethnic groups to certain politicians or even certain types of business leaders.

Application

Do you see that asking the "who" question opens up a wide variety of topics and responses? Pick at least two questions from the above list and begin to ask these questions to parents, teachers, and any mentors you meet with in the next week. Write down notes about their responses. If you learn names or information for follow up, then follow up and read, watch or listen to something about the people or information you learned.

Chapter Seven
What?

The "what" question is where many details can get explained to you. You should be looking for cold, hard facts when you ask this question. Asking "what" allows the mentor to lay out facts and events which can help you to better understand how a chain of events can open doors, close doors or change your life.

When you start a question with "what," give some thought to what you are trying to learn. If you want to know the key thought, idea or action which resulted in success in your mentor's business, ask the question which leads to that answer. If you want to know what matters to a mentor, then ask the "what" question. The key to using "what" is to be pointed and direct. After you ask a good "what" question, you should be ready to take plenty of notes. Here are some examples.

1. "What is your training regimen?" For someone wanting to grow in any type of athletic ability, the opportunity to ask this question of a sports mentor can give precise details for how to accelerate improvement. The way this question is worded is designed to find out specific actions and timetables.

2. "What tool do you use the most frequently?" What if you want to learn carpentry from a master carpenter? While a carpenter may have many tools, what is the one he uses the most frequently? Once you find that out, it is logical to suppose that mastery of that tool will help you establish a good foundation. If you want to gain some measure of respect with that mentor, then start reading everything you can about that tool and begin to practice with it.

3. "What bank (law firm/ad agency/clearinghouse) do you find to be the most helpful to you in your business?" While this is similar to the previous question, what you are looking for with this question is permission to bypass weeks, months or years of trying to find good business partners. Why waste time looking for good people to partner with in business when you can ask a mentor to share the names of their key friends or vendors with you?

4. "If you were stranded on an island for exactly five years with an unlimited supply of food and fresh water, what three things would you choose to have with you?" This is a question which has been asked many times, but it's still useful to have in your list. It helps you to learn what your mentor considers to be vital to his daily work or happiness. If you made a point of asking this question of every mentor, you could end up with a very interesting list of tools, books, or inventions which you can begin enjoying yourself.

5. "What book influenced you the most?" or "What are the names of the three most influential books in your life?" As with the "who" question we ask in order to learn the names of influential people in the life of our mentor, this question is looking for key sources of written information. When a mentor shares the name of a very important book in his life, your next step when you leave him is to go out and borrow, buy or otherwise find a copy of that book and read it. If you ask this question of all your mentors during a program such as 52 Godly Men/Women, you would have enough books to last you a year or two for study and personal development.

6. "What type of training was the most useful to you in your career?" If you want to be a dancer, this question gives you a way to assess which studio(s) might be helpful to you in your own development. If you want to be a pilot, a doctor, a politician or whatever, your mentor in your chosen field can

point you to practical training which can help jumpstart your own career.

7. "What happened in your life which caused you to want to follow Jesus Christ?" When you meet with men or women of character, it's easy to assume they were always that way. The reality is, that is not the case. There are backstories to your mentors which can help you to understand the importance of making a solid commitment to follow Jesus Christ. As you ask this question, you will find that some of your fine, upstanding mentors used to be alcoholics, prostitutes, drug addicts, gang members, thieves or any number of other sordid characters. As you hear their stories, you can discover the life-changing power which rescued them from who they used to be and transformed them into who they are today.

8. "At the end of your life, what are the words you would like to be said about you?" This is the type of question which can cause misted eyes or even tears. It should at the least cause pause for thought and reflection. The answer to this question is a distillation of what your mentor considers to be the most important principle(s) in his life. The purpose of asking this is not simply to be nostalgic. When you hear an answer such as, "I want people to say, 'He was faithful to his wife and family,' then you need to add that to a growing list of character traits which you pursue.

9. "What are two or three pieces of advice which you think would help most any marriage?" The answer to this question can help you begin to sort through your own personal issues. When you hear over and over the same types of answers from diverse mentors, that adds even more weight to beginning to practice what you hear. If you hear from numerous people that you need to be kind or that you need to communicate every day, that should be a primary focus for your own relationship as you develop it. This type of wisdom is gathered over years

and by watching numerous marriages succeed — and fail. You ignore it at your own peril.

10. "If you could go back ten or twenty years, what one change would you make in order to be more successful in your career (or life/marriage/trade)?" By asking this question, you are asking the mentor to share with you what he has learned from trial and error. You may get answers such as, "I would invest in XYZ company" which aren't particularly useful. But you may also get answers such as, "I would get up an hour earlier and pray" or "I would leave work earlier and spend time with my family" or "I would read more books about business management." If you get a less-than-useful answer, you can try rephrasing the question or preface it with something like, "While we all would like to have invested in that company when it started, what one other change would you have made in your life which I could perhaps learn from?"

Application

Find two of the questions above which interest you the most and begin asking those questions to mentors, adults, teachers and even your peers. Write down their answers. Do you see any common themes in their answers? Start making a list of key answers which you want to emulate or begin practicing in your own life.

Chapter Eight
When?

When? This question gets overlooked because it doesn't seem to be as vital as the first two we have studied. But for those who are wise, they understand that sometimes, timing is everything. The same action exercised by the same people at the same place may produce different results depending upon the time of day, the day of the week, or the month, year or even decade in which it is performed.

If you think that life is only about facts and not about having to wait and wait and wait and wait some more, then you have much to learn. Success is not just the product of right actions. It is also the fruit of patience and correct timing. Your mentors can teach you so much about timing if you are willing to ask them the "when" question. Here are some examples of that type of question.

1. "When did you realize you were able to stand on your own two feet without your parents?" Especially for young men and women, this question helps to understand the maturation process and the reality of stepping out on one's own. Often, young people are hesitant to act with boldness because of a lack of clearcut examples which put their own fears in context. By hearing the stories of mentors who understood when they had come of age and were ready for life, it can help to guide or at least smooth the transition from puberty into adulthood.

2. "When did you know it was time to leave your job?" If you are not being fired or forced out, leaving a job can be an extremely difficult decision. But sometimes it's the best decision. By asking this question of people who have made the transition, you can learn to recognize the signs of when it may be time to leave an establishment. As well, it can also

potentially save you from making a bad decision to leave a job too early.

3. "When did you make the decision to start your own business?" As with the previous question, asking this question can help you understand the wisdom and information that a person used in making a decision to initiate a new business. What do you hear him telling you? Did he look at the economic forecast from key research groups? Did he listen to the advice of key people in his own life? Did he look at the market and decide he could get a lead position? All of these tidbits of wisdom can help you in learning to make better decisions yourself.

4. "When did you decide that you were going to pull the trigger?" In this instance, you may be asking the question of a hunter or even a police or military sniper. Either way, this type of question is getting at the heart of a life and death decision. Asking it can help you understand how the person is able to process such a huge decision and to set aside the potential emotional repercussions, even momentarily. Of course, the same type of question could be asked of an athlete: "When did you know you were going to throw the curveball for strike three?" or "When did you know that you were going to choose a running play to win the game on fourth down?"

5. "When did you commit your life to God?" The answer to this question is important in understanding how long your mentor's character has been shaped by his religious commitment. Has he been trained in character development and right living since he was a child? Did a key event bring about this change of direction much later on in life? If you find yourself struggling with your own character and failures, sometimes it is helpful to understand how long another person has been living successfully in those same areas. It can give you hope or incentive to keep trying.

6. "When did you realize that you had made the wrong decision to _____?" The fill in the blank is intended to give you the chance to ask this in context when you hear a mentor speaking about regrets, bad choices or similar actions. Not all bad decisions are readily apparent. The poor investment of time or resources can take years before their waste is understood. Asking this question can help you to glean the criteria which people have found helpful in assessing their choices. It can also assist you in learning that even in the midst of some colossal failures, people can continue to have success in other areas of their lives.

7. "When was the most painful time of your life?" This type of question is good to begin understanding how our lives go through seasons. Whether it is the death of a spouse, the loss of public confidence or a good name, or the failure of a business, pain sometimes comes to stay for a while. If a mentor is willing to share his pain with you, that is a sacred moment. You can listen and learn principles which can help sustain you during your own times of pain — which will come.

8. "When do you get the most accomplished, during the day or night?" Although the world has changed much with the advent of electric lighting and three-shift jobs, most people still live in a morning-person's world. This can be disheartening for the night owls. But listening to mentors describe their "key times" of productivity can be enlightening. One of my mentors told me early during my high school years that he got his best writing done late at night when everyone else in the house was asleep. Hearing that as a young man helped me to understand that not everyone has the same exact time frame for getting his best work done.

9. "When is the best time for a person to marry?" Let's be candid. Most young men and women may not want to hear the answer to this question. But to the few who ask and listen

carefully, the answers you get could help you to avoid a painful relationship. Or, it could help you to better prepare for a really great relationship. Don't be surprised to hear responses such as "when you have a good job and a house" or "when you are able to love someone else without being selfish." Again, the answer to this type of question can offer you wisdom gathered through personal pain or by observing a lifetime of marriages as they succeed or fail.

10. "When will you know that you have succeeded as a parent (or business owner/employer/friend)?" This question is geared to help you understand your mentor's true definition of long-term success. A person can become a parent with a lot less stress than what is required to be a successful parent. The same is true of becoming a successful business owner or spouse or whatever else. The answer to this question can help you understand life goals which are larger in scope than just the immediate and obvious goals. The answers to this question should probably find their way onto yet another list you develop for your own growth.

Application

As with the previous questions, you should find a couple which are particularly interesting to you. As well, you could try going through the list with a mentor or teacher, asking permission to read a list of questions and then making notes of the answers. See how deep you can go with the person in their candor. As you learn to ask this question, write down your observations on what you may need to remember or actions you may wish to take to benefit from what you learn.

Chapter Nine
Where?

The fourth question of the Five W's is "Where?" Where events happen is an integral part of those events. That seems counterintuitive to a generation which spends a good portion of their lives in an ethereal place called cyberspace. But real places are full of history. Good stories always have a place attached to them because history happens in real places.

The Old Testament has an undercurrent of place throughout the books. The idea of "the land" was a major pillar in the understanding not just of life but also of God's covenant with the people of Abraham. Wars have been and will continue to be fought over borders, boundary lines, farms and even the placement of fences.

Places can have an impact on your failure or success. The holder of the high ground has an advantage in battle. The person who rushes the net in tennis has an opportunity to seize the point and maybe the match. Taking the inside route on a defender can open up an athlete for the game-winning pass. Sitting in the front of the class, bus or business meeting can provide an opportunity to step up higher.

Mentors and people in general like to talk about the interesting places they have been. Places change, and their meaning in our lives changes, too. Special places have special meanings for a reason. Ask "where" to find out where you need to be going. Here are some examples.

1. "Where did you meet your spouse?" This question opens up some interesting answers. I've asked this question and

been told everything from "school" to "church" to "in a bar." Either way, the answers are diverse and interesting because they have a story attached to the place.

2. "Where do you sit or stand when you are leading a business meeting?" This question gives you insight into some of the nuances and subtleties of business and human interaction. Does your mentor sit at the head of the table in an obvious power position? Does he sit at a round table to evoke teamwork? Does he stand and walk around the room in order to interact with the attendees? A good follow up to this would be to ask if he always sits in the same place.

3. "Where were you when you felt the loneliest you have ever felt in your life?" This is another good question to evoke a story. If this question were asked as, "When was the loneliest time of your life?" the answer would be different. By focusing on the place, it actually can evoke a plethora of images, sounds and even smells which are all stored in your mentor's memory. The story becomes richer and more detailed because it is grounded in a specific place.

4. "Where is the best place for a midfielder to position himself for a counterattack?" By asking this question, a young athlete is asking for expert advice which will help him to learn how to play better a certain position in a sport. This same type of question can be used for any sport because there are key places in them which the professionals have learned and understand. They can teach you the value of those places if you ask.

5. "Where is the best place for me to begin to network with other people in my career?" Successful professionals all have watering holes, restaurants, guilds or other places they frequent in order to rub shoulders with other professionals. Business deals happen there. Partnerships are formed. Do

you know where these places are? Are they open to you? If so, when will you start visiting those places?

6.   "Where did you grow up?" This is a good stock question used to get to know a bit about a mentor. But if it's used properly, it can help you to learn the type of background and adversity that a mentor had to overcome in order to get to where he is today. Did your mentor grow up in an affluent neighborhood or on the wrong side of the railroad tracks? Did he grow up in an inner city or on a 500-acre farm? It's not uncommon to hear about mentors who grew up in relative obscurity and who have since traveled the world.

7.   "Where did you move to after you married?" This type of question can be helpful in learning some of the key principles for good marital or in-law relations. Some people moved into their family's house. Others moved across town. Some moved out of state in order to establish a comfortable distance. By asking this question and some follow ups ("Did this work out well for you? Did it work out well for your spouse?), you can begin to gather ideas on what has worked or has not worked for people at the start of their marriages. You may hear that one person moved out of state but then realized they missed or sorely needed the support structure of their extended family. You may hear from another who lived next door to family about the grief he endured because of interference. Learn the importance of place in this key part of life.

8.   "Where do you go to relax?" While this may not seem important to you in the early years of your life, this is one of the secrets of living a successful life. The ability to relax is important not just to mental health but also to physical well-being. Successful people usually have one place or a few key places where they go physically in order to back away from the stresses of family, business or life in general.

9. "Where do you go when you are angry (or sad or depressed)?" This question, similar to the previous one, can help you understand the ways mentors use a change of location to deal with negative emotions. Sometimes trouble escalates because one or both parties stay in the same place instead of backing away. Also, it is possible to step out of depression by stepping out of a depressing place into a different location with different sights, sounds, smells or tastes.

10. "Please describe to me where your most enjoyable vacation or mission trip or business trip happened." The mentors you meet with may have a once-in-a-lifetime location which they thoroughly enjoyed. Did they see the changing of the guard at Buckingham Palace? Did they get to walk into a jungle and see gorillas? Did they boat down the mighty Amazon River? You can learn about interesting places you may have never heard of by asking this question. It can give you ideas for your own future trips, or it may open your mind to opportunities to impact the lives of people you didn't even know existed.

Application

Ask two or three of these questions to mentors, teachers, parents and friends during the next week. Be sure at least one of your questions is either number eight or number nine. Based on what you learn from others, begin developing a place you can go to when you experience negative emotions or when you are feeling stressed and need to relax. Try it. Measure the results in your own experience.

Chapter Ten
Why?

The final question of the Five W's is "Why?" You know this question. You asked it of your parents a million times, it seems, when you were 2 or 3 years old. And as you transition through puberty, this question rears its head again as you begin to wonder about the reason for being told to do so many things your parents deem important. So, before we talk about this question in more detail, let's talk about the dangers of using it.

You should not be using this question as an automatic crutch every time you are told to do something. That is actually exhibiting an underlying rebellion against authority. Since authority is ordained by God in order to help preserve families and the social order, ultimately you can find yourself pitted against God asking this question over and over. You don't want to be there. Don't ask me why.

That brings up another point. Sometimes, there is no time to explain, and delaying obedience to a command could cost someone a life. When a battle commander says, "Miller, you take your troops down the left flank and fire like crazy when you see my flare," Miller needs to obey. There could be a wounded comrade needing to be rescued or enemies to be ambushed. In the same way, your parents, mentors and coaches in life do not always have the luxury of explaining everything to you. There are people in authority over you who really do have your best interests at heart. When they give you an order, the way you show appreciation is to obey it without having to ask why.

Psalm 111:10 states that those who obey God's commandments have a good understanding. In other words, sometimes you will never know why until you obey. So, deal with that truth, wrestle with it, cry about it, but accept it. It's scripture. The good news is that living in obedience eventually does bring understanding.

Now, let's talk about proper ways to use this question when talking to a mentor. Here are some examples to get you started.

1. "Why did you choose to go to college rather than beginning your business immediately?" or "Why did you choose to build your business rather than go to college?" This type of question can help you understand the types of preparation people value or even that sometimes an opportunity is in and of itself an educational process. Either way this question is posed, you should be able to glean some pointers for helping you to make a clear decision when you face the same crossroads.

2. "Why did you leave the country of your birth?" Admittedly, this question will not fit all of your mentors. However, you may have opportunity to spend time with people who did leave their home country. That is a huge decision. Finding out why will give you some insight into the types of pressures, national shifts or even the open doors which lead a person to make such a dramatic life change.

3. "Why did you ignore what all the experts were telling you about your idea?" Can you imagine asking this question to Thomas Edison about the electric light? Or can you imagine asking this of any of the famous inventors or scientists in the past thousand years? There are some people whom you meet who understand perseverance and commitment in a way that surpasses everyone else. When you meet someone who has persevered, ask this type of question.

4. "Why do you attend the church you attend?" This question is like a box of mixed candies: you can end up with plenty of different answers. But the point of asking this is to

help you learn to evaluate how to assess where you worship and with whom you worship on a regular basis. While you may end up with some basic answers such as, "I like the pastor's preaching," you may also learn something about their commitment to a group of people through thick and thin — a group of people who are not their blood relations.

5. "Why did you choose the profession you are in?" In Communist countries in the past, the answer would have been simple: I was told what to do. But in many countries, the answer is tied to a myriad of factors. What you are looking for in the answers are pointers on how government policies, economic factors, education, personal talent, persistence, parental influence, mentors or even a childhood dream affect a person's career choice. Hopefully, some of the answers you hear will cause you to examine your own goals to determine if they are realistic or even worthy of your time and effort. It would be far better to have these challenged before spending a large portion of your life seeking what could turn out to be an empty well.

6. "Why did you wait to have children?" or "Why did you have children immediately after marriage rather than waiting?" This is a somewhat personal question, but people on both sides of this decision have their own reasons for doing so. This is a much better question if you can ask someone who has already lived to see their children raised and on their own. The passing of years can change the perspective on this.

7. "Why do you homeschool your children?" Some of the mentors you meet may be involved in the homeschooling movement. While this is becoming more mainstream in the U.S. and some other countries, it is not uncommon to read stories of state or local officials in public education who are still misapplying laws or even bypassing the law to frustrate families who choose to go this route. In other words, the

decision to homeschool a child is a time-consuming endeavor and potentially stressful in interpersonal relationships with family, friends or fellow church members. Asking this mentor the "why" question can open you to a new way of thinking about education.

8. "Why did you leave a good paying job to work in a non-profit ministry?" (You can also reverse this question as necessary.) History records the stories of people who were deemed successful in the eyes of society but who left it all to work with the down and out or the forgotten. The stories aren't always pretty or glitzy. Leaving a salary for uncertainty can cause great stress on a family, and working for a non-profit is usually a lesson in sacrifice. So, why do people do it? Ask. Listen to the deep, underlying reasons which would cause a person to make such a change.

9. "Why do you avoid ____ foods?" Occasionally, you will notice that a mentor makes mention of not eating certain types of food. When he lets that slip, ask the "why" question and fill in the blank with what he mentioned. Being healthy physically is a daily choice and involves being educated about what certain types of food do to your body. While you are learning about all the other topics, find out why your mentors eat the way they do.

10. "Why did you turn down the promotion (or transfer or new job opportunity)?" Sometimes mentors don't leave a job and work in a non-profit. They may be in business their whole life but still avoid making certain career moves which they deem to be too stressful, harmful to their marriage or children, or maybe just too far away from the people and places they love to visit easily. By listening to these answers, you can learn more about placing value on many, many things other than an increased salary.

Application

The "why" question helps you to understand a mentor's heart, his decision-making process and how motives influence reality. After reading this chapter, you can tell your parents that you discovered that "why" is not a four letter word. Then show them that by how you learn to use the word properly. Start asking "why" questions for a specific purpose of learning to understand more about how your parents, teachers and mentors understand their part in the bigger picture of the world.

In conclusion, the five W's will be a staple in your mentoring relationships. Learn to use these questions regularly. Then, listen to the wisdom as the answers come.

Chapter Eleven
The Big H

In our last lesson, we learned about the Five W's. Those question words are "who," "what," "when," "where," and "why." Those five questions alone will open up a world of knowledge to you when you learn to ask them to mentors and the wise people around you. There is another question which is every bit just as important as these. We will call it the Big H. That question is "How?"

How? This word allows a baseball player to describe the secrets behind making solid contact with the ball versus swinging a piece of wood. How? The banker who knows the secrets behind handling money in order to purchase property can educate you with the response to this question. How? The world renowned chef can explain the ingredients and the processes for making an exquisite dish. How? The man who hears from God can help you learn the secrets of hearing God for yourself.

Whereas the Five W's focus on bare facts, the motivations behind the facts, or decision making, when you ask someone a "how" question, your potential for learning is even greater. That is because the question "how" is intended to lead to an answer which explains a process. A good answer to this question can include a set of steps which you can reproduce. It's very common for people to spend thousands of dollars to attend seminars in order to learn the answer to just one "how" question. Yet, if you meet with the right mentors, you may be able learn some of the same processes from them directly.

After asking someone "how," you need to sit down, be quiet, listen and take copious notes. As with the previous questions, let's look at some real-world examples.

1. "How do you pay off a loan quicker?" If you ever borrow money in your lifetime, there are easy-to-understand steps for paying off a loan early. Once you learn these steps, you will be surprised at the amount of money you save in interest costs. If you have never learned this, you need to ask someone who can teach you these steps.

2. "How do you train for higher level sports?" During his high school years, my oldest son had an opportunity to meet regularly with a trainer who had worked with several large programs, including a national title football team and the U.S. Olympic Team. This man was living in our small town. He knew quite a bit about how a young man could advance his weight training and pack on the muscle. My son was able to ask many "how" questions and benefit from his years of experience.

3. "How do you buy a piece of real estate with no money down?" Most people don't know that this is even possible. Yet, there are people around the world who know the secret of this and who generate wealth by using the reproducible steps they themselves were taught.

4. "How do you select a mentor (or trainer)?" If you really respect a person's wisdom or character, why not ask this question? It is entirely possible to align yourself with someone whose influence will do more to discourage you than to help you. I saw that with another man whom I paid to try and help one of my children with a particular athletic skill. There was no doubt that he was a great athlete, but it became apparent that he wasn't capable of assessing, analyzing and then teaching someone else who did not learn the same way he did. As you grow, you need to develop the ability to spot key traits in people which indicate their value to you as possible mentors.

5. "How do you choose the right place to seek advanced education?" Not everyone needs to attend a traditional

college or university. Apart from ending up with a mountain of debt, you may not be any closer to pursuing your career goals. A good mentor can help you discover your gifts and talents, and a really good mentor can help point you to one or more particular paths which will help you develop those talents.

6. "How do you raise children?" Admittedly, raising children well is a lifelong pursuit which is demanding and would cover more books than most people care to read. Yet, if you look at a mentor's grown (or growing) children and really like what you see in their attitudes and character, then that mentor has something which he can share with you about what he is doing right with his children. If you learn only one new principle or truth which you can put into practice with your own family, it's certainly worth asking "how."

7. "How do you write a good term paper (or poem or book or magazine article or short story)?" One of the mentors who spoke to our middle school group of boys told the story of making the transition from high school to college. He had been told that he was a good writer, so he enrolled in university to take more English and writing courses. His professor took his first paper, graded it, returned it to him and said, "You really aren't a good writer." While that was true, she didn't stop there. She said, "But I can help you to become one." For the next four years, he spent one evening per week at her home. He would eat a meal with her family and then spend an hour or two learning more about how to write. When he asked her how he could ever repay her, she gave him a simple answer, "Write a book." He did. In his instance, a mentor found him and taught him "how" to acquire a skill which is still influencing his career over thirty years later.

8. "How do you create a pie crust which is so flaky and delicious?" Some people just know how to cook. But how they

cook, bake, or barbecue something is entirely reproducible. There is nothing magic about their hands or even their measuring cups. If you find someone willing to answer this question, you can advance your ability to create extremely tasty food by learning reproducible steps for yourself.

9. "How did you learn to hear the voice of God?" For people who believe in God's ability to provide personal direction in their lives, learning to hear His voice is a major step in their spiritual growth. I've met people who seem to flow through each day with a clarity of God's direction and His will, and I know people who seem to struggle with the basis of their faith. Are there reproducible steps you can learn which will help you mature in the spiritual dimension of life? If you believe in the God of the Bible, the answer to that has to be "yes." That means there are people who can help you learn those steps or principles.

10. "How do you pray?" This last question brings to mind the very simple question which the disciples asked Jesus, "Lord, teach us to pray" (Luke 11:1). They were asking, "How do you do it?" These were grown men who had jobs and families but who realized that they had never learned an important skill. Instead of pretending they knew what to do, they asked "how." Jesus took time out of His admittedly busy schedule to teach them, and, through their writings, hundreds of millions of people since then.

So in our own lives, it requires humility to admit that we do not know everything. It also requires about a half ounce of common sense to admit that. The sooner we get over whatever pride may be hindering us from asking a mentor to teach us a truth or a skill, the sooner we can begin learning the deeper secrets of a successful life.

In conclusion, the Big H is one more tool to add to your

collection of questions. Getting your questions answered may require an investment on your part, not just of time but also money. The question you have to ask yourself honestly is this: "How much do I really value my own growth and development?" Your answer may lead you to sacrifice free time, all your available money and even time from family or friends in order to gain wisdom and knowledge. The people living at the pinnacle of success have one statement for you to weigh: "It's worth it."

As you begin to learn week by week how to use the questions we have been learning, do not underestimate their power. They are like keys to ancient doors behind which lie riches and treasures beyond your powers of imagination. The author and poet Rudyard Kipling summed up their importance in the following poem:

> *I keep six honest serving-men*
> *(They taught me all I knew);*
> *Their names are What and Why and When*
> *And How and Where and Who.*

Application

Think about some of the things you would like to learn. Write down one which is relatively easy to learn. Find someone (parent, teacher, mentor, relative, friend) who can teach you that skill. Ask them an appropriate "how" question. Take the steps they give you and practice what you have learned. If you are having any difficulties, go back to the person and ask for additional information or clarification in order to perfect what you are learning.

Chapter Twelve
Setup and Follow-Up Questions

Early on in the process of my children meeting with mentors, their questions tend to be lighter in weight. As they meet week after week, they begin to learn to ask some deeper questions. One thing I tell them to watch out for is the simple "yes" or "no" question: "Do you like your job?", "Have you ever had tough times in your life?", or "Do you enjoy working overseas as a missionary?" When they suggest a question like this to add to their list, I simply say, "What kind of answer does that question expect?" After a pause, they may answer, "Yes or no." At that point, I ask them, "How could you rephrase the same question so that you get a story or a more detailed answer which could be useful to you?"

These types of questions can give you some basic factual knowledge about your mentor, but they do not necessarily give you any additional wisdom to apply to your life. Remember that your goal in meeting with mentors is to gain knowledge which you can apply to your own life. Some of that knowledge you may not have a chance to apply for twenty years, but if you learn it, it will be available to you when you need it. One way to accomplish the goal of getting applicable knowledge is to have some basic questions which set up some follow-up questions in order to find out a particular set of information. Let's look at some examples.

1. I recommend that you always ask if the mentor really likes his job. That's a "yes" or "no" question which is usually not helpful unless it is accompanied by a follow-up question. In this instance, if the mentor says he does like his job, the follow-up question would be, "What do you like about your job?"

The reasoning behind his answer can help you to understand how your career choice can affect your family or your personal well-being.

2. A different way to approach it is to ask the question, "What do you find personally fulfilling about your job?" This seeks to find some of the motivations behind the mentor's career. The answers you receive to this question would typically be different from those from the first question. When you begin your own career, you will discover that doing work which uses your gifts and talents is far more important than simply making money. If you do not have a job which scratches the itch of doing what you are gifted to do, then you will always be searching for ways to use your gifts outside of your job.

3. Eventually, you will probably meet a mentor who answers that he does not like his job. When you do, ask him why he is still working the job if he does not like it. It's important for you to realize the motivations which drive people to stay in careers which are not fulfilling. Debt could be one of those motivations. Or the mentor may have chosen a major in college at random based on impulse rather than a well-ordered plan. Can you learn from a mentor's career mistakes in order to avoid the same problems?

4. One of the best follow-up questions is the one you were told over and over again not to ask when you were a child: "why?" When you ask a mentor if he attended college, if he answers in the affirmative, then ask him, "Why?" If you ask him what he majored in, he might say he majored in business. Ask him, "Why?" You might be surprised to discover that some of your mentors majored in a certain area because they really didn't know what they wanted to do by the end of their sophomore year. They had to declare a major and simply chose something because it was the path of least resistance or was popular or any number of other reasons. Another good

follow-up question in this type of scenario is to ask what he would change about those decisions if he had it to do over again.

5. If he says he didn't attend college, then ask him, "Why not?" His answer may be that he didn't have the money and did not want to go into debt with college loans. Or he may have chosen not to attend college because he had a job opportunity awaiting him after high school.

Hopefully you will realize that some of your mentors made mistakes and some bad choices because they did not have mentors of their own. Many of the people in my generation went to college because we had been told by educators that if we wanted to be successful, we had to go to college. No one laid out any of the other paths to success, which can include apprenticeships, career mentoring relationships, trade schools or simple entrepreneurial options.

6. Another excellent follow-up question is "how?" As we talked about in the last chapter, this question is designed to give you reproducible steps in order to obtain similar results in a given area. A similar way of asking this question is, "What steps can I start with in order to make progress on this goal?" A good mentor can tell when you are at step number nine when you really think you are at step twenty-four. While it may be humbling to be told that you are not as advanced in a skill as you think you are, it can also free you up to focus on what you really need to work on. It also allows you to avoid unnecessary failure which is more likely to result from attempting to operate at a level higher than your actual skill.

A very simple example would be for a pro basketball player to tell a young high school or middle school player that they need to focus on dribbling with both hands. The young person may believe that practicing three-pointers is the most important skill to work on. But for a professional who makes his living by using a wide range of athletic skills to tell the young player this, he is freeing him up to become a better athlete at a more normal pace. In this example, the fact is that more time in a basketball game is spent dribbling the ball than shooting it.

Let me add a note about processing negative feedback from mentors. If the mentor you meet with doesn't know what level you are at or does not know how to move you from one level to the next, keep asking other mentors until you find someone who can. One of my children was told by a person we were paying for specialized training that the child did not have the ability to learn a particular athletic skill. It really affected the child emotionally. As the parent, I had to come alongside that child and say, "Let's put things into perspective. This so-called professional coach does not know how to get you to move to the next level. Rather than admit that, he is putting the blame on you. What we need to do is to find someone who knows what your next step really is." That helped the child to process that situation and make the determination to not give up on a goal. Eventually, that child was able to find someone who knew a particular step which needed to be fixed and then could practice it over and over. That made the difference, and it also proved the previous person wrong.

7. Have you ever really considered quitting? What were the things you did in order to persevere? This pair of setup and follow-up questions is designed to give you some practical steps you can use to avoid defeat and learn to handle negative emotions.

8. If you were able to go back and raise your children all over again, what would you change about how you raised them? What type of feedback have your own children given you about your success as a parent? These questions are part of everyday life all over the world. It's amazing that so

few people have ever asked this question of anyone given that so many people become parents. By asking these two simple questions, young parents can prepare for the process of raising their own children with less careless errors.

9.   How do you balance organism versus organization as a leader of a community, church or small group? What has not worked for you as a leader in this area? This question (and the next one) came from an adult who would like to find a mentor who can help him grow his church. These questions are examples of more direct and specific inquiries. They can help you to avoid pitfalls as you have opportunities to serve in leadership roles.

10. What are the keys to successfully launching small groups in a church or organization? Is there a particular size of a church which is too small for having small groups? These very pointed questions are examples of finding out specialized knowledge from someone who has succeeded and has overcome obstacles in the journey. Note the second question: it shows some knowledge of the fact that the goal (small groups) may be obtainable only at a certain point in a church's growth.

When meeting with mentors, sometimes you will receive an answer which is incomplete or useless in helping you make your own progress. When you do, ask your question again in a different way. Do this until you get an answer which allows you to determine steps you can take to move forward.

For instance, if you want to be a professional soccer player and you have asked a retired player what you can do to reach you goal, he might say, "Just get out there and play!" That doesn't help you. Ask the question again in a different way: "At my age, what is a particular skill I should focus on in order to prepare for the next level of soccer?" Or you could ask if there are particular schools or programs you should attempt to join in order to be better prepared. The question you want to ask yourself with every mentor is, "What is the gem or nugget which I can take away from this meeting which will get me one step closer to my goal?"

Application

Practice asking some setup and follow-up questions with some of the adults or mentors available to you. Try to focus on getting information which you can apply in the next few days.

Chapter Thirteen
The Protocol of Questioning

Right after a natural disaster, with millions of people watching on TV, the reporter stood beside the mother who had just lost all her children. Looking into the camera, he said, "We are here live at the scene of the devastation. This poor woman has just lost her family." Then he took the microphone, and before thrusting it in front of her face, he asked, "Tell us. How do you feel right now?"

That offensive scene has been played out on TVs around the world year after year after year. So often, I just wish someone would take the microphone, shut off the camera and send the reporters packing. The person has just gone through horror and has lost family and property. And for the sake of ratings only, the question you ask is, "How do you feel?"

While we are learning that questions are one of the keys to growth, we must understand that there is a basic set of protocol to follow when we ask questions. If you learn to follow this protocol, you can avoid unnecessary embarrassment and anger in your relationships. You also will be more likely to actually get the information you are seeking without being shut out or even physically attacked.

The first rule is to be sensitive to the other person's pain. Everyone has experienced disappointment and loss of some kind. Some have experienced great loss. To begin probing at the source of the pain while it is still fresh is like tearing a scab off a wound: it prevents healing from taking place, and it brings a fresh round of pain to the person who is already hurting. If a person has just lost a family member within the past two years, he may not be ready to talk about that. If he has had a colossal failure in the past year or so, he may still be reeling from that and not even have perspective on it himself yet.

Pay attention to the circumstances. What have you heard or been told about this person? What have you read in the news? Are there photos of children with flowers around or in front of the photo? Is there a general feeling of sadness? Is there a white patch of skin where a wedding ring used to be?

Another rule to follow is that when you ask questions, ask to learn and not to accuse. "Why did you wreck the car and kill your family?" assumes willful intent. Asking, "How did the wreck happen?" is a totally different way to try to find out the same information. Think of the times your parents have done this the right way and the wrong way. "Johnny, can you explain how the milk got on the ceiling" is different from "Johnny, why are you always making a mess?" Maybe, just maybe, it really was the cat's or dog's fault just this once. "Why do you think you were accused by everyone else?" gives a person a chance to respond from his humanity and his side of the story.

A different rule to remember is to simply ask permission. Before you talk to mentors, it's a good idea to say, "When we talk today, is there anything which you consider 'off topic' for questioning and conversation?" If they answer that in the affirmative, then avoid those topics no matter how much you want to know or how much the topics may include one which you really wanted to ask. Asking permission allows you to respect another person's basic right to privacy. If there are things I want to share with you, that's my choice. If there are things which I choose to keep from you, that is also my right and my choice.

Finally, in all your questions, show basic human decency. Is the person you are asking questions to just an object who is supposed to answer and teach you things? Or is he a human being created in God's image? If the latter, then treat him like you would want to be treated.

Application

Before you meet with your next mentor, do a bit of research with people who know him. Ask them if there are any sensitive areas you should consider avoiding. When you meet with the mentor, ask if there are any topics which they wish to avoid in your conversation.

Chapter Fourteen
Questioning Authority

"Never question God!" That was the advice given by one old lady I met in church. While it sounds spiritual, it doesn't actually line up with what happens throughout the Bible. Many women and men in the Bible and in history have wanted to know "Why?" The basic issue here is whether it is right or permissible to question authority.

Before you ask the first question to an authority figure, you need to understand the culture you are in. There are some countries in the world where questioning a leader is considered to be treason punishable by death. In these countries, you may wish to read this lesson and then hide it in your heart for some other place or some other time. I have had the privilege of working with pastors and leaders in Africa. Some of these countries still imprison people for publicly questioning the big political leaders. If you are in a tribal culture in a country ruled by a dictator, it doesn't matter if you are an American with a Bill of Rights. You're not in Kansas anymore. Know your context and respect it.

Regardless of where you live, the first principle of asking questions of someone in authority is to remember that you must respect authority. Scripture tells us that authority is ordained by God. Because of this, if we adopt a rebellious attitude toward authority in general, we are, in fact, resisting God. If you know in your heart that your attitude isn't right, then you probably shouldn't be asking questions of someone in authority.

A good rule of thumb in assessing this is to talk to people in private whom you know and respect. Ask them if your question is valid. Ask them if your attitude is proper. Listen to their feedback. (Keep in mind that if you only seek counsel from your peers, they may have the same question, but they are willing to use you as the sacrificial lamb by encouraging you to be the one to actually do the questioning.)

The second rule is to ask after obeying. No one in authority wants to have an order delayed because someone just doesn't understand why. Psalm 111:10 states that those who obey God's commands have a good understanding. In other words, if you want to understand God's ways and His reasons, then you have to obey Him first. This is true with parents, employers, military leaders and any other level of authority in our lives.

You will run into this principle throughout your life. Some leaders or authority figures may really be wanting to help you grow, but they will test you before spending much time actually teaching you. They want to find out if you are really willing to apply what they tell you. That's fair. After all, you are asking them to invest their time — their most valuable asset — in you. Some authority figures will give seemingly boring or routine assignments for days, weeks or even months before beginning the process of explaining the what, why, or how of their expertise.

If you are the person "stuck" in this type of relationship with a leader, you can get frustrated and give up, or you can trust that they have a better idea than you do about the processes needed to help you develop. Instead of asking "why" out of frustration, focus on doing your best work on whatever task they assign. If you do this, some answers you will figure out on your own. If you try to shorten the process through impatience, chances are, you will lose ground with your leader and never learn what he wishes to teach you.

The third rule is to ask in humility. How you approach authority is extremely important. If you approach authority with an air of pride, insolence or entitlement, then you can expect to be rejected — or worse. Americans especially might struggle with this since we are taught the importance of our rights from childhood. Asking a question in humility means that you recognize that you do not know everything and that your rights are not always as important to others in the light of a bigger picture.

Body language is an important part of this. The old adage "no one sits higher than the king" is a good rule to remember. For instance, don't walk into a leader's office uninvited and put your hands on his desk while he is seated, lean over him and begin shouting, "Why are you having me do boring tasks?" Compare that picture with being seated in a chair across from the leader, leaning forward in your chair with attentiveness, taking notes on what you are being asked to do, and then repeating the instructions for clarity. A leader is more likely to accept, "May I ask a question, sir?" from the second person.

The fourth rule when questioning authority is to ask to learn. Authority must clearly know that you are wanting to understand their purposes or decisions in order to be able to better anticipate their needs in the future. If we take seriously the command to serve others, then make it clear that you want to ask questions in order to serve better. Consider this example: an apprentice is learning to perform maintenance on a piece of dangerous machinery. The trainer tells him, "Before you shut the machine down and begin your maintenance, you have to lock out the controls with this locking mechanism." It would be fine for the apprentice to ask several questions of the trainer. "How do I perform the locking steps? What could happen if I forget to do this? Have any accidents occurred as a result of someone not locking out his machine properly? Are there any warnings or indicators to remind me of locking out the controls while I am still in training?" These types of questions let the trainer know that the apprentice is listening, cares about what is being taught and wants to learn.

Fifth, consider that it is wise to ask questions of authority in private. The same question asked in public or in front of even a third person might cause you to be punished, whereas if you ask it in private, you might find an answer. The reality is, sometimes leaders deal with pride issues just as much as everyone else. They don't like being made to look bad or being put on the spot any more than other people. Also, at times they are compelled to protect the position they are in even if they have little interest in protecting their own personal reputation. Questioning a judge while he is sitting on the bench can show disrespect not just for the person but for the law itself.

Sixth, you should understand that there is a time to ask questions and a time to not ask questions. As we mentioned in an earlier lesson, when a leader in a war situation gives an order, he expects it to be obeyed immediately without question. So, in your own life, don't ask your questions in the heat of the moment or when someone is counting on you to perform an action. Do it first. Ask later. If you had the opportunity to watch two great chess master dueling, you would not ask, "Why did you move that piece there?" in the middle of the game. The duel is occurring first in the mind and only secondarily on the game board. Concentration is required, and the strategy is kept as secret as possible. After the game is played out, the masters may feel free to comment on the "why" of the game.

Finally, when you question authority, you should be prepared to accept the consequences. Proverbs 20:2 says that the king's anger is like a lion's roar and that angering a king puts your life in danger. If you ask your questions the wrong way, at the wrong time, in front of the wrong people or with the wrong attitude, it could cost you your job, your position, your chance for promotion, your scholarship or even your life. So, questioning authority is something which you can do. But you need to tread very, very carefully.

Application

Set aside time with parents, teachers or mentors and ask them this question: "Have you ever questioned authority in your life, and, if so, what were the results?"

Chapter Fifteen
Mining for Gold

So far, we have looked at different types of questions to ask. We have discussed the Five W's, the Big H and given some guidance on how to approach people for questions. As you begin asking questions to mentors, your experience will be similar to the three travelers we learned about who picked up the rocks in the riverbed. You do have to do some work to reach out and get the jewels of wisdom which your mentors have to offer, but often it doesn't require a great amount of effort.

However, if you want to pursue the deeper truths which your mentors have learned, you need to compare that to mining for gold. Gold, like wisdom, is usually found buried deep down. History has shown that most of the world's gold supply comes from gold mines which require mining for the ore. In the same way, some of the best information you will glean from your mentors is the wisdom you get from digging.

When you study about gold mining, one of the things you learn is that gold is very often buried under at least 50 feet of sand, dirt, and loose rock called overburden. In order to get to the gold, you have to start shoveling away dirt. You have to pull out rocks. You have to remove loads of sand. And you have to do this over and over and over again. Does this sound like a long, hard process? It is. But the people who do this are convinced of one thing: the gold is worth it.

That's the way it is with digging for wisdom with mentors. You can't expect to get the deepest and best wisdom without spending significant time with a mentor or without doing some good, hard digging yourself. What does this mean practically? It means that you have to begin to look at asking questions as a multi-step process. Just like the earth doesn't give up its precious ore by you simply treading upon it, you shouldn't expect a mentor to share his deepest truths with you when you have shown no diligence to find them.

What you learn in this chapter should be seen as a beginning. It may take you weeks, months or years to get a good grasp on how to craft a set of questions which you can use at will. Better yet, what you really need to aim for is to learn how to ask questions in the moment, feeling out the person you are interviewing as well as any audience which may be present. This takes practice and an attention to detail which is honed by trial and error. The main point is to understand that much wisdom is never learned because it is left under the surface. Sometimes the wisdom is ten questions away from you. Sometimes it's only one more really good question away.

Occasionally, you may leave a meeting with a mentor and have an unsettled feeling or a sense of dissatisfaction, the sense that there was more to be learned, that somehow you missed something deeper. When that happens, you should spend some time in reflection and ask yourself, "What could I have done differently? How could I have asked my questions differently? What questions were fluff, and could I have dropped them in order to have more time to ask the ones which mattered most?" You should also ask your parents, teachers or the mentors closest to you to try to help you to understand what you could have done better.

Right now, we are going to look at a sample set of questions which are designed to dig deeper and deeper. This is part of the curriculum which we have taught our middle school and high school youth. Also, in the Spring of 2018, I had the opportunity to teach a course on Mentoring to a group of pastors and teach from Central Africa as part of a leadership training program. I taught these questions as part of that course. The next day after covering these questions, we had an unique opportunity to interview an entrepreneur and business owner from Lusaka, Zambia who happened to be visiting the training facility. I took the exact list of questions below and worked through them one at a time. The answers he gave were very insightful, and the leaders enjoyed what they learned from him. When the interview was over and the guest had departed, I asked the leaders, "Do these questions work?" They gave a resounding, "Yes!"

Therefore, take some time as you read through the list of questions below. These questions deal with the people who influenced your mentor. Pay attention to the progression of these questions. Make a copy or add them to your own notebook of questions which you use.

1. "Who are some people who influenced you?"

2. "Out of those people, which one had the most impact on your life?"

3. "Why would you say that person was the most influential?"

4. "What lesson did you learn from that person?"

5. "When did you learn it? (How old were you?)"

6. "How did you put that lesson into practice?"

7. "What obstacles did you encounter when you tried to put that lesson into practice?"

8. "How did you overcome them?"

9. "What advice would you give me at my age to benefit the most from what you have learned?"

Do you see how we started with the easy questions and then began working our way through the dirt, sand and rocks? While it may be interesting to know those who impacted your mentor, you may never be able to meet those people. Then, when you narrow it down to the most influential person, it's the same. You may never meet that person. He may be dead or on the other side of the world. But even if you can meet that person, what you are really trying to find out is what your mentor learned from his mentor.

By asking about his age, you are trying to determine if there is anything particular about his age which mattered. Is this a lesson you could learn at your age? When you ask how he put it into practice, you are trying to learn reproducible steps you can take to implement the same lesson. The questions progressively dig deeper in order to arrive at truth which you can use.

Do you think this set of questions will work for you in your culture? I had asked that question to the African leaders I mentioned earlier. Each day I would bring nationally or internationally recognized speakers into the classroom for question-and-answer sessions to talk about their own mentoring experiences. When I asked this set of questions from start to finish to the businessman, the students knew what I was doing because we had just gone over these questions. Now they were seeing them put into practice, and they realized that these questions would work for them in an African context just like they do in other places.

It is a fact in mentoring relationships that sometimes a person will share deep truths with you only if you display a determination and drive to get to those truths by deeper questioning. Jesus himself said, "Do not cast your pearls before pigs" (Matthew 7:6). If a person has no interest in wisdom, why should a mentor waste his breath on him? By learning to dig for gold, you become the type of person who receives wisdom, because you will become the type of person who knows the process of how to find it.

One more important note about gold. Once you find gold, it is usually in a vein. That means there is a whole bunch more where that came from. When you tap the deeper wisdom and insight from a mentor, there is no telling what you will learn as you continue to explore, dig and find the rewards. Dig for gold!

Application

Add the list of questions above to your notebook. Ask each of the questions in the order listed to a teacher, a mentor and a parent. Write down the answers. Are there any follow up questions you think should be added? If so, write them down. Now start to develop your own set of questions (five or more) which dig down on a particular topic or point of interest for you. Ask your teacher, parent or mentor for feedback on how you can improve your own questions.

Chapter Sixteen
Drilling for Oil

In our last lesson, we talked about mining for gold and how that represents a different approach to asking questions. There is another type of gold we want to discuss today: black gold. That's one of the nicknames for oil.

Oil is much more plentiful than gold, but it can require much more work in order to obtain it. Whereas gold is often found in veins underneath the surface of the earth in relatively shallow depths, oil is buried much deeper. The world's deepest gold mine is around 13,000 feet below the surface. That's 2.5 miles or 3.9 kilometers. But that's still shallow compared to the deepest oil well. It is over 40,000 feet below the earth's surface! That's 7.5 miles or 12.5 kilometers down below.

Here's a fact: you don't simply walk out your front door one day and just happen to discover oil 40,000 feet below the surface. With the technology available now, companies are using satellite imaging, infrared technology, geological surveys, massive computer systems and just about anything they can harness in order to search for the next big oil deposit. That is called research. If you want to find oil, you have to do a lot of research before you ever drill.

Let's talk about that in relation to mentoring. If you realize that you lack wisdom in a certain area of your life, or if you are trying to acquire a certain skill or develop an ability, you should spend significant time in research. What does this not mean? It doesn't mean that you get on the Internet and type in a search term once and click on the first link. While that can be helpful, you are never going to be an expert on anything of significance simply by doing that — unless you want to be an expert on clicking on the first link you get. The reason experts have their information posted on the Internet is because they have spent hours, days, weeks, months, years and even decades trying to become the best at something. If you want to begin to have that type of success, that type of "oil" in your own life, you have to begin to spend time finding out where to drill for that oil.

Using the Internet can be helpful at times to get a broad overview of a topic. Mostly, you should use it to begin searching for the names of people who are the experts. What you very often will find is that these experts have taken the time to write down their knowledge in books. Once you get the names of those books, you buy them or you check them out at a library. Or you find someone who has a copy and borrow it. Then you read it, as quickly as you can with as few interruptions as you can in order to maximize your initial learning. It's best if you own it, whether it is printed or digital, because then you have it to use as a reference whenever you need it. And you can mark it up with a real or digital highlighter when you come across key points. Then you read it a second time, a third time or however many times it takes in order to assimilate the knowledge recorded in the book.

When companies begin searching for oil, they spend significant amounts of time in their research. Don't just buy one book and focus only on it. Almost anything worth learning or any skill worth developing in your life will usually have a multitude of books and materials available for you to increase your education.

Did you know that people routinely spend $1,000, $5,000 or even $10,000 to attend seminars where they can listen to experts speak on a single topic? This happens all the time in the world of finance. People spend large amounts of money in order to learn how to buy and sell real estate, how to protect their assets using the legal system, or how to promote their business properly. Usually, the people who attend these seminars already have read plenty of books and are at the point that they know that they need to learn more. By reading and studying for weeks or months before attending, they are better prepared to ask the kinds of questions which will make the money they spend worthwhile.

Don't you think that it is worth as much time and money (or more!) to learn how to have a happy marriage? Don't you think that the secret of raising your future children is more important than just learning how to make more money which you can't take with you? If you believe that, then you won't have any problem spending your money to listen to people who can teach you those truths. You won't have any problem buying books, audio or video libraries or any other materials which can help you learn those truths.

Plus, if you really believe it, then you will spend time reading, studying, researching and preparing for the time that you have with a key mentor. You may have time for only one question. If you have spent the time preparing, then you will be able to ask the kind of question which drills straight into an oil well of wisdom.

Remember that wars have been fought over this resource called oil. People have died to find it. They have died to extract it. They have died to claim it. And they have died to control it. All of this is for a substance which isn't eternal. How much more should we value wisdom?

Jesus said that "since the day of John the Baptist until now, the kingdom of heaven suffers violence, and the violent take it by force" (Matthew 11:12). Was Jesus telling us to promote violence? No. What this saying means is that the type of person who lays hold of the treasures of the kingdom of God is the type of person who is willing to fight the hardest for those treasures. Are you willing to fight your own laziness in order to gain the best treasures? Are you willing to fight your desire to play games or watch movies in order to spend time studying and researching and seeking wisdom? If you are not willing to give everything you have in order to gain the deep riches of the kingdom of God, then don't complain when others own them. You have your chance, right now, to make choices which will affect the rest of your life. (That truth is a free barrel of oil for you.) Listen to that truth again: you have your chance, right now, to make choices which will affect the rest of your life.

Listen to the wise man in Proverbs 3:13-15:

> *Happy is the man who finds wisdom, and the man who gets understanding. For its profit is better than the merchandise of silver, and the gain is better than fine gold. She is more precious than rubies: and everything you can desire are not to be compared with her.*

The deepest wisdom requires the hardest work. Choose to begin to walk down the path that leads you to the oil.

Application

Spend some time reflecting on an area of wisdom or knowledge which you lack but which you really want to understand better. If possible, do an Internet search to try to find the names of men or women who are recognized experts on that topic. Do more research to see if they have written books. Pick out one or two of those books and buy or borrow them. As you read the books, take notes on key points which you learn from those experts. Make a list of questions you would like to ask those experts if you ever have the chance. Based on what you have already learned in this process, try reaching out to those experts (or others) by mail, e-mail, social media, telephone or face-to-face to ask one or more of your questions.

Chapter Seventeen
Digging a Well

Gold is valuable. Oil is the lifeblood of world commerce. But there is something which a man would give all his gold and oil in order to obtain. Do you know what that is? It's water, the most plentiful resource on the planet in terms of sheer volume.

Do you believe me? All you have to do is get the richest man in the world into the middle of the Sahara desert for a couple of days. If he has no hope of getting out alive, and you show up with a few gallons of water, you can bargain with the upper hand. Why? Because even though precious stones, precious metals and other things are considered valuable, we do not have to have them in order to live.

So, the question you need to ask when it comes to your own growth and development is, would you rather dig up some occasional gold, drill for an oil well, or have an ever-available fountain of water? Before you answer, think about the fact that life itself is full of desert places. You will have times in your life when you feel as if the whole world is against you. What good is oil and gold then?

How do you get an ever abundant supply of water? By digging a well. Back in the olden days, wells were dug by hand with very crude tools. Some of them were very wide and very deep. They were often lined top to bottom with brick to prevent them from crumbling and stopping up the flow of water.

Finding a good, solid long-term mentoring relationship is just like digging that well. Rather than looking at the person as someone who can supply you with a few nuggets of gold or some barrels of oil, finding a long-term mentor means that you can go back to that person over and over again, day after day, week after week, year after year in order to keep asking for wisdom and perspective on the life issues you confront.

Asking someone to be your mentor is a serious proposition for both sides. You need to research your mentor as much or more as you would when prospecting for gold or locating an oil field. Some water is bitter, other water is salty, and some water is polluted. You don't want to have a mentor who is going to be offering you muddy water. But there are people who are committed to serving Jesus Christ who are willing to spend time with young men and women. Their lives exhibit purity and a single focus to please Him even in the midst of what may be a busy life.

Your challenge over the coming weeks, months and years is to actively look for and seek out those men and women who can guide you into your next level of growth. Some mentors may be in your life for a year or more. Others may span decades of your life.

You have a good selection of tools to help you in asking the mentor questions and asking them at the right time. But what you need next is a mentor. Begin to pray and ask God to bring the right person or persons into your life. Don't expect fifty. If you can find one good mentor, that is a wellspring enough to get you started in strong character development and growth.

For a more detailed resource on how to find mentors, please look at my guidebook for parents. You can find more information at 52GodlyMen.com.

When you narrow down a list of potential mentors, you need to approach them in the proper way. What you don't want to do is come across as a tick or a leech. Most people have enough business in life to not want to add more things unnecessarily. If you are dealing with truly wise people, then they are going to scrutinize anything which demands more of their time, because they will be the kind of people who understand that time is a gift from God to be used properly. So, whether you write a formal letter (recommend), an e-mail or make a phone call, you should begin by stating what you admire about the person. Tell him that you have been watching his life and appreciate that he is wise, makes good decisions, has a successful business, raises his children well or whatever it is which is significant to you. Then, state that you have been praying that God would help you to build a team who would be willing to provide you with guidance and feedback on your life decisions. Tell the person that you would like to spend time with him on a routine basis. State that you would be open to anything which fits his schedule and note that this could include hiking, talking over coffee, showing up and simply watching him work or whatever he would be willing to do. Ask him if he would be willing to pray about this decision and then contact you. After you communicate, if you don't hear anything back in a week or two, then follow up with another letter or call. Be willing to follow up three or four times before moving on.

Once you get a positive response from one or more mentors, be willing to be extremely flexible. If you have a chance to hang out with friends or spend time with a mentor, tell your friends that you need to reschedule. If you want to truly grow in a mentoring relationship, it is up to you to do everything in your power to make it happen. Some of the best results will come from simply spending an hour per week just talking about life. If a mentor is willing to let you come to his job site, then dress appropriately and be prompt.

Finally, it is important to note that safety is not something you hope for. It needs to be planned. If you have vetted your mentors properly, you shouldn't have an issue. However, it's worth stating that meeting in public places or with more than one person is a good idea. If a mentor begins to talk about sexual topics on a regular basis, consider ending the mentoring relationship. It should go without saying that a mentor who tries to touch you physically, especially in private areas of your body, should be dropped like a hot rock and should be reported to authorities. Also, if a mentor begins to bring in ideas which you know are in direct contradiction to the Bible, then you should end the mentoring relationship. If a mentor isn't wise enough to submit to the Word of God, then he really isn't wise at all.

Application

In the past lessons, you have learned quite a bit about how to make the most out of mentoring relationships. Now, put it into practice. Find a mentor. Get started. Grow.

Chapter Eighteen
Putting It All Together

Over the past several lessons, we have explored a variety of guidelines on how to make the most of your time with mentors. We have looked at the basics of greeting someone and the importance of listening. We have explored a graduated process of beginning to ask questions and then learning to ask better and deeper questions of mentors. We have highlighted the significance of developing a relationship with a mentor (or mentors) which will be longer term than just one or two meetings.

Where does that leave you? The answer to this question is based on where your heart is. If you have a genuine interest in growing, getting better in skills or abilities, in gaining wisdom for how to deal with life's challenges and a true passion for excellence, then the path is pretty clear. You will begin to look at the people you meet not just as random human beings but as potential mentors. You will ask questions of them in order to determine their depth of wisdom and understanding, and you will be evaluating whether or not they would be the type of mentor you need in your life. You will also begin to reach out to these mentors and ask them if they would be willing to spend some time with you for the purpose of helping you become a better person (or better athlete or better businessman, etc.).

If, on the other hand, you are satisfied with mediocrity, the path is simple. Don't do anything. You can do just what people used to write down in my high school yearbook: "Stay the way you are, and you will go far in life." While that sounds warm and fuzzy, it's seldom true. Successful people keep growing. They keep learning. They change. They confront obstacles, adapt to the times where necessary and maintain a rigorous dedication to obtaining their goals. If you don't want that, don't do anything. Stay the way you are, and you will easily obtain a mediocre life. You will be like the masses. You can live your life in debt, depression, and with the standard complaints of your generation. Or, you could even potentially lose ground, beginning a downward slide and ending up in worse shape than you ever thought possible. It is really up to you.

The challenge for you today and tomorrow is to commit in your heart and mind to take action. The first step is to be humble enough to admit that you don't know everything and that you can use instruction. The second step is to identify the person(s) who can help you obtain that knowledge. The third step is to reach out to potential mentors and ask if they would be willing to help you. The fourth step is to meet with them, ask questions, listen and take notes. The fifth step is to follow through; take the actions necessary to put into practice what you have learned. The sixth step is to repeat the above process as long as you live.

One final point to make is that after you have begun growing and developing, you must look for people who need your help and offer it to them. You are where you are today in a large part because of the contributions of other people into your life. You owe society itself a great deal because of that. Also, wouldn't it be so much better if instead of you having to find mentors, they would find you? What if everyone in your community were wise and always took the time to seek out young people and help them through their decisions and struggles? If you think that would be a good place to live, then help to make that a reality by becoming the person who seeks to mentor others.

I hope you have enjoyed these lessons. I hope they have made you begin to think more clearly about your interaction with mentors. Be willing to send me your feedback through the years as you take these lessons into your life. I would be delighted to hear how you have used them to grow and what wisdom you have learned in the process.

Acknowledgments

As always, I appreciate the men and women who are willing to meet with my children as part of their 52 Godly Mentors experience. You deserve more recognition than I can give you in a short space. Thank you!

I am also grateful to Deana, my wife, who is willing to use her extensive editing skills to make all of my writings better.

I also remember the times Rev. Dollas Messer spent with me during my teenage years, helping me to learn the principles of discipleship. He also was a good example of someone who taught that we should be willing to submit all of our questions to God and His sovereignty whether or not He chooses to answer them during our lifetime.

Comments

Did you enjoy this book? If so, we would really enjoy hearing from you. To share a comment on this book or a story about how it helped you, send us a note at: askingforwisdom@thompsonpublishers.com.

Please visit us on the Internet at thompsonpublishers.com where you can find more resources.

To support the author's work in leadership development, training, mentoring, evangelism, and writing more books and curriculum, visit this URL:

> https://www.walkwithgod.com/giving

Errata

A list of corrected errata is maintained at:

https://www.thompsonpublishers.com/askingforwisdom

The publisher requests that any additional errata be sent via the form on that page.

Other Books in The Mentoring Revolution Series

Nurturing Your Child with Mentors: This book gives parents an understanding of the numerous ways a child can benefit from meeting with mentors. Examples from the lives of children who have met with mentors are included in each chapter.

How To Be a Mentor for a Day: This book is designed to help men and women understand how to prepare for a day or part of a day mentoring a young person. The chapters include easy-to-follow instructions. It has received great reviews from past and future mentors as a valuable resource in the preparation process.

Bonus Content

Now available in print or ebook: Shattered by Petra Thompson. Contact your local Christian bookstore or Thompson Publishers.

Thompson Publishers
thompsonpublishers.com

Shattered
Copyright © 2019 by Petra Thompson

Requests for information should be address to:
Thompson Publishers, PO Box 2605, Cleveland TN 37320-2605

ISBN: 978-1-64407-006-2 [print]
ISBN: 978-1-64407-007-9 [ebook]

All rights reserved. No part of this book may be reproduced, stored in a retrieval system, or transmitted in any form or by any means -- electronic, mechanical, photocopy, recording, or any other -- except for brief quotations printed in reviews, without the permission of the publisher.

Scripture taken from the New King James Version®. Copyright © 1982 by Thomas Nelson. Used by permission. All rights reserved.

Cover design Craig Thompson © 2019.

Printed in the USA.
First printing.

Prologue

I'm an atheist. Well, I haven't always been one. I used to be a Christian. Back when my family was together, and happy, or so it seemed. Back before we found out that my dad was a druggie after he purposefully took an overdose and died. Then my mom got addicted to alcohol and started abusing us kids. So, don't I have a good reason for thinking that if there were a God, then He would've taken better care of me? See, I was raised a Christian because my mom and dad were raised as Christians. They got saved at an early age and went to church; but when I was about six, they decided that they could do better on their own, so they left the church and forgot about God. That was right after I had gotten saved. But then they kept doing these terrible things, and I figured, well, if they can do those things and call themselves Christians, then I don't want to be one.

There are three of us kids. There's my older brother, Jackson, who left home at fifteen because he was tired of being kicked around. Some role model. Next, there's my older sister, Kimberly, who's still around but takes out all her problems on me. She has a bunch of friends and is super popular—and loves taunting me about it. She's not an atheist, but she's definitely not a Christian. Then there's me. Brown hair and brown eyes, I look like an average, normal girl with a normal family. That's all lies. I'm like a book. You can look at my cover and assume so much, and unless you start to read me, I appear normal to all who look at me.

I live in a small house, in a small neighborhood, near the middle of town. The house may be considered decent-sized to some, but it's too crowded for me. In it, there's my mom, my sister, my cat, and my grandmother, Eileen Morgan, who just moved in with us, making the house seem even smaller. Plus, she's been a so-called Christian practically from the womb, so I get sermons from her all the time. "Go to church, stop sinning, you shouldn't hang out with those people, they're bad influences..." Blah, blah, blah. She's such a hypocrite. She doesn't even go to church. Sometimes I wish I could just run away. But, if I had, I wouldn't have met that one girl, on that one day, and had that one conversation.

I was at a Christian summer camp one day, forced to go by my grandmother, and was trying to eat my nasty lunch. I had to eat the cafeteria food because there was no other option—other than starving to death. I recognized some people from school, mostly people I didn't hang out with. At school, I hang out with almost all the groups: the jocks, the pops, the nerds, the normals, and even a few of the bads—though very few of them are actually my friends. I hang out with every group but the

Christians. Or the "Jesus jerks," as I like to call them.

So it caught me off guard when one of them, Tina Lankford, came up to me while I was finishing eating and said, "Can we talk? God's got something to say to you."

I was dumbfounded. I didn't believe that there was Someone up there, much less Someone who would want to talk to me. I didn't want to listen to her, but I couldn't help myself. I was super curious to find out what this girl thought a non-existent God was "saying to me." She led me out of the cafeteria to a picnic table and sat down.

"I'm going to get right to the point," she said. "God told me last night to talk some sense into you, and I'm gonna do it. You have been away from God too long. You know, deep down, that there is a God up there, but you have told yourself lies for so long that they have infested your heart and mind. The message God said to tell you is this: 'I am here. You can't see me, and you don't try to listen to me or feel me. You are blinded by fear and hatred. Seek me. Find me through others until you are ready to accept me again yourself. I have been standing at your door knocking for years, but you have drowned me out. I am finally going to make Myself heard. Stop blaming your mother, your dad, your brother, your sister, and your grandmother. Open the door.'"

In shocked silence, I felt my eyes water. I didn't even know this girl, but the message she gave me was directly for me, and it hit home.

"I thought about this all night," she continued. "I think God wants you to go on a mission to find godly women. Women who seek Him. Women who want to share their story so you can find yours. Women who will talk to you and listen to you. Women who will be your friend. So I challenge you today to find one godly woman every week for the next year. Ask them questions to find out for yourself if there is a God. Will you take the challenge?"

I stared, mutely watching her eager face. Then, hardly realizing it, nodded. "I will," I said.

She smiled, a joy that I couldn't explain lighting up her countenance. "I know you won't regret this!"

I got up from the table and left, feeling warmth inside that I hadn't felt in years. It was like a drop of water on my parched lips.

So that's how I got stuck with this crazy "mission" that I have committed myself to for the next year. I don't know what I was thinking when I agreed to it. But, at least I'll have a good excuse to get out of the house more often. I may give up after a few weeks, but who knows? Perhaps by the end, my cover will have changed, and my story, too.

Chapter One

A frustrated sigh filled the space in my drab, colorless room. I'm supposed to be meeting with a godly woman this week, and the week is almost over. I groaned as I remembered my conversation with Tina. I racked my brain, trying to imagine someone I could meet with. If only Tina had suggested someone then. As I mentally went through, for the millionth time, the limited list of godly women I knew, a light flashed before my eyes. In annoyance, I glared at the now burned-out bulb and then stomped down the stairs to grab a new one for the ceiling fan.

After finding the bulb underneath the bathroom sink, I stopped outside the bathroom to look at the photos on the wall and stared blankly at the picture of our smiling family. It's amazing how much looks can be deceiving. Two participants of the picture have left. My dad left permanently, and my brother left indefinitely. Just then, my grandmother yelled from the living room.

"Brie, please get me a glass of water with four cubes of ice, no straw, and a slice of lemon. I have a headache and getting up will only make it worse."

I rolled my eyes as I clumped over to the yellowed cupboards in the kitchen to grab a glass and fill it up, tempted to tell her that if she could yell that well with a headache, then she ought to get it herself. I was always fetching this or that for her. That's me. Brie Thompson, the family's servant. My actual name's Hazel, but when I was three I snuck out of my bed at night and went into the kitchen to get a snack. The only thing I could reach in the fridge was some Brie cheese, so I pulled it out and began to eat it; however, my family heard me and came into the kitchen to see what the commotion was about. When they found me sitting on the floor eating an enormous amount of cheese, they called me Brie, and the nickname has stuck. I don't even bother introducing myself as Hazel because people have called me Brie most of my life. I've sort of adopted it as my real name. Even some of my teachers call me Brie. Whenever someone calls me Hazel, they normally have to say it twice because I'm not used to being called that.

Upon delivering the requested item to my lazy family relative, I paused as I left the room. An idea was forming, and I could feel it coming up fast. I looked at my grandmother once more, and it popped into my head. I could see if my dad's mom could meet with me. I knew she was Christian, and I figured she would be the best choice to start out with, especially since I hadn't seen her in ages. When Dad died, everyone on his side of the family was ignored, and my mom constantly declined invitations from them until they gave up trying. I didn't agree with my family's decision at the time, but as I grew older, I just accepted the fact that I could do nothing to change anyone's mind on this. I grew bolder with the idea and decided to contact her, looking through an old address book for her number.

When I hesitantly called her, I expected her to hang up on me; however, that wasn't what happened. I was rather shocked when she greeted me with surprise and cordiality. Once I told her the purpose of my call, half expecting her to laugh as if I were a crazy dodo, she readily agreed, telling me that she had been praying for an open door to communicate with my family. After we had formulated to meet the next day, I hung up and went to tell the shocking news to my mother.

I gingerly creeped into her dark bedroom, stepping around piles of dirty clothes, shoes, and empty bottles. I tiptoed over to her bed and shook her cautiously. When she finally woke up, she groggily glared at me and demanded the purpose of this disturbance of her beauty rest. I could tell she was still suffering from a hangover and mumbled that I was meeting with my grandmother tomorrow and wondered if she could take me. She rolled her eyes.

"Your grandmother is in the next room. Why do you need someone to walk you over there tomorrow? You could just talk to her now." I was getting nervous about where this was heading.

"Not your mom," I said in a timid voice. "Dad's mom." She stared wide-eyed at me before bursting into laughter.

"You actually talked to that woman? Have you been drinking?" She erupted into another peal of laughter. I glared at her, wishing she would magically understand.

"I just talked to her on the phone. She wants to meet with me tomorrow." Mom stopped laughing and cocked a sassy eyebrow at me.

"So regardless of my explicit restrictions, you purposefully decided to override my authority and communicate with his family. You, my dear troublemaker, are quite the audacious one. You actually thought that someone related to your father would stick true to her word and actually see you? That would be a first."

I had tilted my chin up higher and higher as she kept talking; however, once she insulted my grandmother, I had had enough. "Pardon me for breathing, but I do believe that as her granddaughter, I have an obvious right to visit her, whether you say so or not. And, contrary to popular belief, she will indeed stay true to her word, if I have any say in this unfair matter." I gazed boldly into her taunting eyes and cocked my own sassy eyebrow right back at her.

"Fine. I will prove to your ignorant soul that she will not do as she promised. I will personally drive the forty-five minutes down to her house just so I can watch the expression of defeat on your face when you realize the cold, hard truth."

I smirked, knowing that she had just talked herself into a trap. Feeling victorious, I gracefully turned on my heels and glided out of the room to replace the light bulb.

The next day, I was genuinely surprised to see that my mom actually followed through with her promise to take me. I lightly bounced into the passenger seat and sat waiting for my mom to turn on the ignition. She was silent on the way down, either from going over the ways she could rub it in my face if I were proven wrong or from the realization that she was talked into a trap by a few simple words and a challenge from a so-called rebellious teenager. I gloated on the fact that she would have to drive away without me once we got to the house.

Once we arrived at the white, ranch-style house, I got out nervously. What if my mom was right? I timidly knocked on the door and clasped my hands behind my back. The door opened and before me, in the flesh, stood the woman I hadn't seen in years.

"Hello, Grandmother."

"Brie?" She paused. "Do you still go by that, or have you changed it back to Hazel?"

"It's still Brie," I said.

"Alright then, Brie." She gave me a bear hug and welcomed me inside. Before heading into the house, I triumphantly looked over my shoulder at my mom as she backed out of the graveled driveway. I couldn't see her expression, which was probably a good thing. Grandmother inquired if I were thirsty—which I was—and she offered me a seat on the couch. She came back from the kitchen with a glass of orange juice and sat down on a chair opposite me.

"You have no idea how happy I am to be meeting with you today! I haven't seen you in forever!"

I smiled sheepishly and couldn't think of anything to say. She wasn't at all like my mom made her appear to be. In fact, she was quite the opposite.

"I was trying to figure out what to do with you today, and I wondered if you would like to do a flannelgraph story from the Bible, since you used to love those as a kid. I don't know if you still love them because I'm not quite familiar with your recent interests." She added the latter part with a knowing look followed by an understanding smile. "But I know that isn't all your fault."

I was shocked. Was someone actually not blaming me for something? Everyone always blames me and makes it seem like it's always my fault. I quickly hid my shocked expression and quickly chose the story of the ten plagues from Exodus because I was most familiar with it. I hadn't been to church in years, but I figured that I would remember it well enough.

"When you tell a flannelgraph story," she began, "you have to orderly prepare the pieces and set up all the backgrounds." We went into the room where she kept her materials, and we started going through the pieces. I never knew how hard it was to set up a flannelgraph story. We had to get all the plagues, all the people, all the props and food, and all the scenery, even if we were showing the piece for only a split second.

As I was looking at the flannelgraph pieces, I suddenly had a flashback to when I was a little kid, sitting on a tiny carpet circle in children's church, listening to Grandmother teach the story of the crucifixion with flannelgraph. I was already a Christian at the time, and I sat there with tears streaming down my face as I listened intently to what they had done to Jesus. Grandmother was such a wonderful teacher that I felt like I was actually there. I'm surprised that I remember that snippet of my history, since I laid to rest the faith issue long ago. Yet, I also remember that that was the story that made the children's director mad because showing "gory" pictures to children was not acceptable, so he forbade Grandmother to show the pictures of the crucifixion. As a result, Grandmother stopped teaching there. I didn't understand why he thought it was such a big deal. Even as a young kid, I had already seen plenty of movies with death scenes in them, and I know that other kids had, as well. The flannelgraph pictures were nothing compared to that!

"There's a little book on the dining room table from which you can read the story of the plagues," she remarked, drawing me back to the present, as she set up the easel I would be using for the story. "It tells you the order of the plagues and the background of the story."

I read it to refresh my memory so I wasn't babbling the whole time. I was amazed at what the Egyptians went through during the plagues, and I could see tidbits of the story that had never caught my eye before. For example, the people stayed in the same place for three day during the plague of darkness—although I didn't think that they sat in the same exact spot for three days. That would be a little tough on the rear end. I set up the background for the story and began. I was a bit shaky at first but became more comfortable as I neared the end. The longer I told the story, the more respect I had for my grandmother—how she had to prepare for each story in advance then set up all the pieces every week for the Bible story at church for children who likely had no clue how much time and effort it took her. I know I sure didn't.

"That was wonderful!" Grandmother said as I finished the story. "You were very good." I was startled at the praise. I rarely heard anything complimentary from anyone, so to hear that I was actually good at something was a mind-boggling affair.

Once the story was over, we put all the flannelgraph away.

"Would you like to get some fresh air?" Grandmother said. "I would love to show you my flowers." I nodded, and she smiled wide as she led me out the door to her flower garden. She showed me her rhododendrons and geraniums. As I walked through the roses and wildflowers, her two favorite flowers, my sock caught on one of the many thorns from her rosebush. As I knelt down to free my foot she laughed and remarked,

"Growing up, my sister and I weren't allowed to wear socks because they were too 'worldly.' We had to wear nasty pantyhose." I looked at her in incredulity. Socks were considered worldly? Drinking, drugs, and R-rated movies maybe. But socks?

She wasn't finished. "And on top of that, we weren't supposed to go to baseball games or the theater. The first movie I ever saw in the theater was an army flick that my aunt convinced my parents to let my sister and me go see. My uncle was in the army at the time, so my aunt said that we might see him in it. We didn't, but I was able to see my first movie in the theaters."

"I had no idea that the church was so strict back then!" I exclaimed. "Nowadays people go to see movies all the time!"

"Yes, church was pretty strict in my days. Things have changed a lot over the past few decades, however, and that's why you see people doing things that wouldn't have been acceptable at all in my time." We walked back inside and sat down in the living room to continue talking.

"Well, I guess the best place to start," Grandmother began, "if I were telling you my story, is with my name. On my birth certificate, my name is Daisy Naomi Ruth Ridgeway, but when I got my driver's license, I dropped my first name and went by Naomi."

"That's cool that you just up and changed your name," I commented. "Kind of like me. Isn't that a Bible name?"

"Yes! It comes from the Book of Ruth, where Naomi leaves her homeland because of famine, her husband and sons die in the foreign land, and then she returns to Israel with her daughter-in-law Ruth. I was a lot like my namesake growing up. I was born in Buford, GA but then moved all over Georgia. Being a pastor's kid, I didn't stay in one place for a long time."

"I remember," she continued, "the time my dad was pastoring a church in Lafayette, GA. We didn't really like living there, but we had to stay. One night, my dad had a dream that we had moved to Fitzgerald, GA. When he shared it with us the next morning, we didn't believe him; we figured the dream was merely a product of his desire to leave. However, after breakfast, he got a phone call from a leader of the denomination that he was being sent to pastor in Fitzgerald. We were pretty shocked."

I was skeptical. God gave him a dream that he would move? God giving people dreams was only for biblical people like Jacob or Joseph or Paul, not ordinary, modern people. I sighed inwardly. I had figured that I would probably get a sermon while meeting with Grandmother. At least she seemed legit and not a hypocrite, like all the other people I knew.

"When I was seven," she went on, "my church was having a revival, and it was summertime in Georgia so the doors were wide open in the church. When the altar call came, I was ready to walk to the front and get saved, but the devil told me that I shouldn't go up because I didn't have any shoes on and people would laugh at me. Well, I didn't go up, and so I didn't get saved. Four years later, two women, Ms. Peacock and Ms. Roach, were speaking in tongues, and the interpretation of it was that the shades of darkness were falling and that Jesus was coming back. Well, that scared me good because it was nighttime, and it was dark outside, making it all the more real. I went down to the altar and didn't leave until I was saved and started speaking in tongues."

"After I got saved, other Christian kids and I would have prayer meetings at the church. We would meet to pray and read the Bible. Becoming saved was one of the most important decisions I've ever made."

The most important decision ever? I was surprised.

"An important lesson I learned growing up," Grandmother continued, "was that you don't mess with the Lord's business. A neighbor that went to the same church as us came over one day and asked my mom if the church could have one of our chickens for the chicken dinner they were hosting to raise money. My mom didn't want the church to kill one of her laying hens, so she said no. Later that day, she went outside to check on the hens and found one of them dead. That's when I learned that you should never mess with the Lord's business."

I couldn't imagine why her God would want to kill one of her hens! I mean, couldn't He just have found another chicken somewhere else? That seemed very vindictive and controlling. Feeling like Grandmother was starting to talk too much about God, I decided to shift the conversation to a safer topic. "What did you like to do when you were my age?"

"I loved to play on the swings, as well as play house, hide and seek, tag, hopscotch, and dolls. I still have a doll from my childhood that's over seventy-five years old!"

I looked at her in surprise. She would keep a doll for that long? I couldn't think of anything that I still have that I played with when I was young—and that wasn't too long ago.

"What do you like to do?" Grandmother asked me.

Her question took me aback. She seemed genuinely interested in me. My brain raced as I tried to think of something I liked to do.

"Well, I love to read books. I always have quite a bit of free time on my hands, since I'm not on a sports team or anything. I can't wait until I'm old enough to get a job and make my own money. Then I'll not only have money to spend on things I think are important but I'll also fill up that time slot with something productive instead of being made to do menial chores because 'idle hands are the devil's work,' as my grandmother so fondly puts it."

"Well, if you grew up in my time, you wouldn't have to wait very long to get a job," Grandmother inserted. "My first job was in a department store at age thirteen. It didn't pay as much as young kids get paid today, but the money went further. The first time I earned what I thought was a lot of money was when my dad said that he would give me five bucks if I could learn a song on the piano. To you, five bucks might not be much, but back then, it was a lot of money. I wanted that money, so I learned a song to play at church. Once on stage, I sat down and promptly forgot where to put my hands to start the song! My brother had to come up on stage and show me where to put my hands, and then I was able to play the song. I bought a jacket with the money I earned from that." I smiled somewhat ruefully, thinking that I would probably forget how to play in front of everyone as well. Just then, I looked at my watch and gasped in horror.

"My mom is going to be here in four minutes," I said, in a slightly worried tone. Mom had probably been fuming when she saw that not only was I spending the day with Naomi (because she did, in fact, stick to her promise) but that she would have to spend time in town finding things to do before coming back to get me because she was wrong about my Grandmother. I doubted that she would be happy, so I was dreading the trip home. It would be almost an hour of either her shrieking made-up lectures to save face or deadly silent rage, like an ominous fog that covers a ghost town, and you don't know what's in it or what will emerge.

I shuddered.

Grandmother stood up. "I'm so glad that you were able to come, darling. It was fun seeing my precious granddaughter today. You've made my day shine."

I warmed at the compliment and dropped my head shyly. "Thanks. It was enjoyable being able to spend time with you because I was expecting a somewhat different reception, since my mom always pushed you all away."

"Well, if I didn't love God and put God first, then who knows how I might have received you? Those are the qualities of a godly woman, you know." I bobbed my head up and down for lack of words.

"Other qualities of a godly woman are knowing and loving the Lord, knowing the Word and practicing it, giving of herself and her time, dressing to honor the Lord, and exhibiting the fruit of the Spirit in her life."

Just then, my mom arrived. I peeked hesitantly out the window to the car and did a weather evaluation. An ominous fog look was upon her face, and I knew it would be a long forty-five minutes. I gave Grandmother a big hug and walked out the door. The trip home was anything but pleasant, and I seriously considered jumping out the window and walking home.

I talked with Tina the next day and told her whom I had met with and how it went. She told me that it was good to start with family members first before looking for other options. She said that if I needed suggestions, she had a few ladies in mind she could set me up with. I thanked her, still a little uneasy about my promise but willing to give it a shot.

As I lay in bed that night, I thought about how strange it was that I didn't remember how nice my grandmother was. I guess time can make people forget many things. Anyway, one down, fifty-one more to go. I don't know what will be at the end of my journey or what my perspective will be, but I know that it will be a challenge week by week; and by the end, I will at least have met fifty-two new women who hopefully will have given me tons of different views about life.

TO READ MORE, PICK UP YOUR COPY OF *SHATTERED* TODAY.

www.ingramcontent.com/pod-product-compliance
Lightning Source LLC
Chambersburg PA
CBHW052105070526
44584CB00017B/2349